# Debbie Bliss
# *Kids' Country Knits*

## More than 30 original patterns for newborns through age 5

ST MARTIN'S PRESS

NEW YORK

**Library of Congress Cataloging-in-Publication Data**

Bliss, Debbie.
    Kids' country knits/Debbie Bliss
p.    ;  cm.
    ISBN 0-312-09837-5  :  $17.95
    1. Knitting-Patterns.    2.  Children's clothing. I. Title. 93-4033
CIP
TT825.B564    1993
746.9'2—dc20

First Edition: 1993
10  9  8  7  6  5  4  3  2  1

First published in the United Kingdom in 1993 by
Ebury Press
Random House, 20 Vauxhall Bridge Road, London SW1V 2SA

Photography by Sandra Lousada
Designed by Jerry Goldie
Styling by Marie Willey

Typeset by Textype Typesetters, Cambridge
Printed and bound in Italy by New Interlitho, S.p.a., Milan, Italy

# Contents

# Introduction

I have had great fun working on the designs for my latest collection of knits for children. The images of the farmyard and the countryside, from plump pigs to hens with their chicks, conjure up such nostalgic memories of childhood, images which my own children love today. I have visualised the animals in a variety of stitches and styles, nestling among cables and bobbles in arans, or walking across fields of fairisle. There are also soft toys which I hope will appeal to adults and children alike, and novelty slippers. I have designed all the garments to have a generous fit, but as actual measurements are given for each pattern, readers can choose the size they prefer. In terms of the knitting skills required, the designs range from the simple to the more challenging, offering plenty of choice for knitters of all levels of expertise.

*Author's Acknowledgements*
I would like to thank the following for their invaluable help – Gisela Blum, Lynda Clarke, Miriam Hudson, Penny Hill, Isabel Kemp, Maisie Lawrence, Frances Wallace, Betty Webb, and Fiona Eyre for her moral support and for contributing the Mexican Sweater and the Milk–Maid Sweater.

I am especially grateful to Tina Egleton for her technical expertise and pattern checking, Sandra Lousada for her beautiful photography and commitment to the project, Marie Willey for her brilliant styling, and Denise Bates, my editor, for her tremendous support throughout.

I would also like to thank Heather Jeeves, for being an exceptional agent.

Debbie Bliss

# Basic Information

## ABBREVIATIONS

**alt**-alternate, **beg**-begin(ning), **cm**-centimetres, **cont**-continue, **dec**-decreas(e)ing, **foll**-following, **g**-gramme, **inc**-increas(e)ing, **in**-inch(es), **K**-knit, **m1**-make one by picking up loop lying between st just worked and next st and work into the back of it, **mm**-millimetre, **patt**-pattern, **P**-purl, **psso**-pass slipped stitch over, **rem**-remain(ing), **rep**-repeat, **sl**-slip, **st**-stitch, **st st**-stocking stitch, **tbl**-through back of loops, **tog**-together, **yb**-yarn back, **yf**-yarn forward, **yon**-yarn over needle, **yrn**-yarn round needle.

## NOTES

Figures for larger sizes are given in ( ) brackets. Where only one figure appears, this applies to all sizes.

Work figures given in [ ] the number of times stated afterwards.

Where 0 appears no stitches or rows are worked for this size.

## YARNS

All amounts are based on average requirements and should therefore be regarded as approximate. Use only the yarn specified if possible.

If, however, you cannot find the actual yarn specified, you can substitute a yarn of similar weight. Make sure that the substituted yarn knits up to the tension specified in the instructions (see below).

It is always best to use the yarn recommended in the knitting pattern instructions. Addresses for Rowan Yarns are given on page 80. If you want to use a substitute yarn, choose a yarn of the same type and weight as the recommended yarn. The descriptions of the various Rowan yarns are meant as a guide to the yarn weight and type (i.e. cotton, mohair, wool, et cetera). Remember that the description of the yarn weight is only a rough guide and you should test a yarn first to see if it will achieve the correct tensions (gauge).

The amount of a substitute yarn needed is determined by the number of metres (yards) required rather than by the number of grammes (ounces). If you are unsure when choosing a suitable substitute, ask your yarn shop to assist you.

## DESCRIPTIONS OF ROWAN YARNS

Cotton Glace – a lightweight cotton yarn (100% cotton)
approx 112 m (123 yd) per 50 g (1¾ oz) ball
Designer DK – a double knitting (US worsted) weight yarn (100% pure new wool)
approx 115 m (125 yd) per 50 g (1¾ oz) ball
Donegal Lambswool Tweed – a 4-ply (US sport) weight yarn (100% pure new wool)
approx 100 m (109 yd) per 25 g (1 oz) hank
Handknit DK Cotton – a medium weight cotton yarn (100% cotton)
approx 85 m (90 yd) per 50 g (1¾ oz) ball
Wool and Cotton – a 4-ply (US sport) weight yarn (50% superfine botany wool/50% Egyptian cotton)
approx 120 m (131 yd) per 40 g (1½ oz) ball

## TENSION

Each pattern in this book specifies tension – the number of stitches and rows per centimetre (inch) that should be obtained on given needles, yarn and stitch pattern. Check your tension carefully before commencing work.

Use the same yarn, needles and stitch pattern as those to be used for main work and knit a sample at least 12.5x12.5 cm (5 in) square. Smooth out the finished sample on a flat surface but do not stretch it. To check the tension place a ruler horizontally on the sample and mark 10 cm (4 in) across with pins. Count the number of stitches between pins. To check the row tension place ruler vertically on sample and mark out 10 cm (4 in) with pins. Count the number of rows between pins. If the number of stitches and rows is greater than specified try again using larger needles; if less use smaller needles.

The stitch tension is the most important element to get right.

*Cardigan and Baby Blanket*
SEE PAGE
36

*Duck All-In-One*
SEE PAGE
38

*Garter Stitch Jacket with Hat and Hens*
SEE PAGE
*42*

*Cow Cardigan*
SEE PAGE
43

*Tartan Sweater
with Chick*
SEE PAGE
44

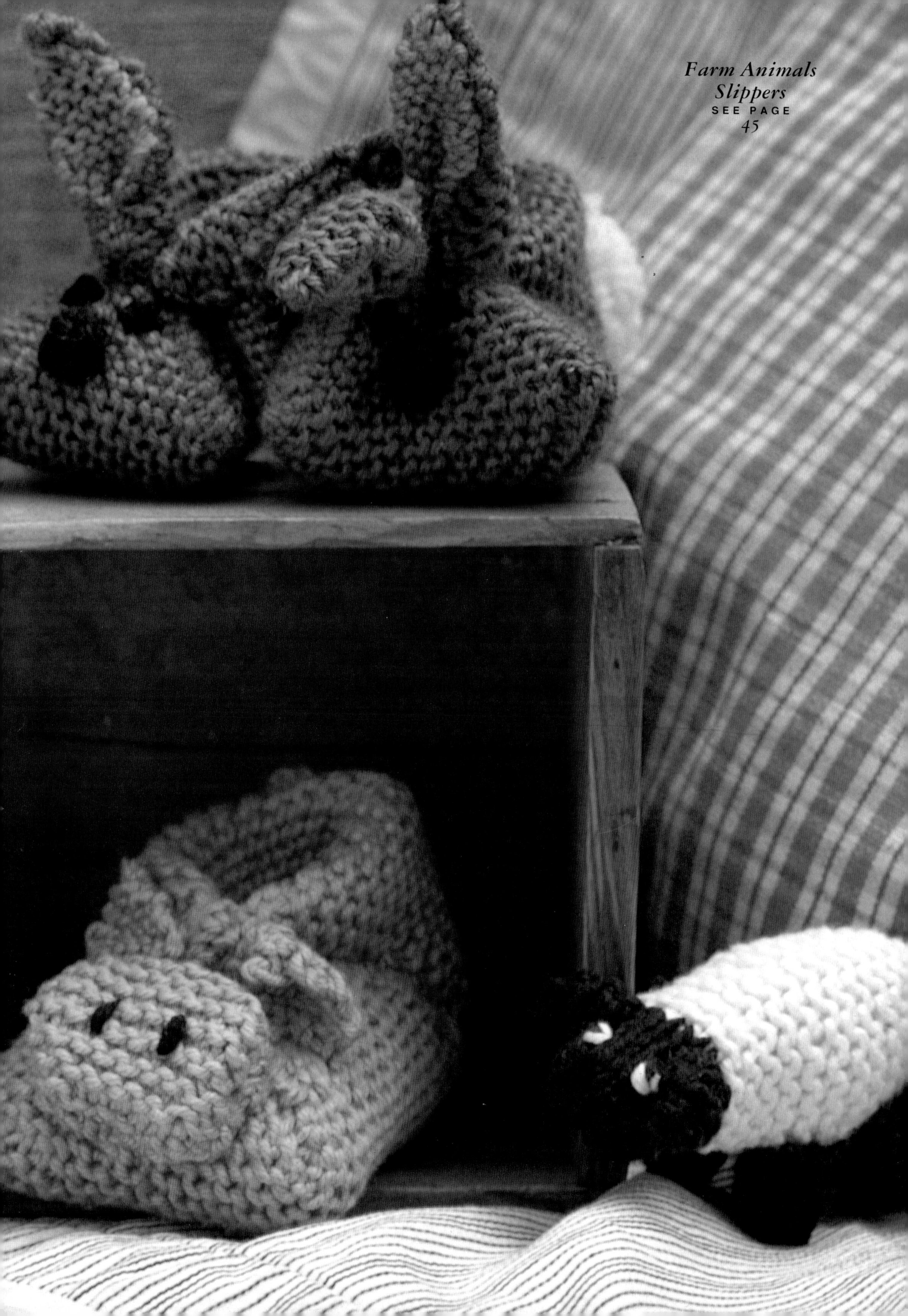

*Farm Animals Slippers*
SEE PAGE 45

*Sailor Collared Sweater with Duck Motifs*
SEE PAGE
46

*Sheep Waistcoat*
SEE PAGE
47

*Aran Sweater
with Farmyard Panel*
SEE PAGE
48

*Cotton Smock*
SEE PAGE
*49*

*Cable Sweater*
*with Chicken Panel*
SEE PAGE
51

*Cow Sweater*
SEE PAGE
53

*Hen and Chick*
*Cardigan*
SEE PAGE
54

*Farmyard Picture Book Sweater*
SEE PAGE
55

*Mexican Sweater*
SEE PAGE
58

Patchwork Sweater
SEE PAGE
60

*Knitted Toys*
SEE PAGE
61–65

*Farmyard Jacket*
SEE PAGE
66

*Duck and Sheep*
*Fairisle Cardigan*
SEE PAGE
68

*Double Moss Stitch*
*and Cable Jacket*
SEE PAGE
69

*Wheatsheaf Sweater*
SEE PAGE
70

*Tunic with Pig
Motif*
SEE PAGE
72

*Cricket Sweater with Cows*
SEE PAGE
73

*Hearts and
Hens Sweater*
SEE PAGE
74

*Sampler Sweater* SEE PAGE 76

*Milk-Maid Sweater*
SEE PAGE
77

*Alphabet Sweater*
SEE PAGE
78

# Cardigan and Baby Blanket

See Page 6

## MEASUREMENTS
### Cardigan

| To fit age | 4–9 | Months |
|---|---|---|
| Actual chest measurement | 60 | cm |
| | 23½ | in |
| Length | 28 | cm |
| | 11 | in |
| Sleeve seam | 18 | cm |
| | 7 | in |

**Pram cover** 54 cm × 69 cm/21¼ in × 27 in

## MATERIALS
**Cardigan** 4 × 50 g balls of Rowan DK Handknit Cotton in Cream (MC).
1 × 50 g ball of same in each of Brown, Red, Blue and Yellow.
**Baby Blanket** 7 × 50 g balls of Rowan DK Handknit Cotton in Cream (MC).
1 × 50 g ball of same in each of Brown, Red, Blue and Yellow.
Pair of 4 mm (No 8/US 5) knitting needles.
Medium size crochet hook.
4 buttons for Cardigan.

## TENSION
20 sts and 28 rows to 10 cm/4 in square over st st on 4 mm (No 8/US 5) needles.

## ABBREVIATIONS
**Ch** = chain; **dc** = double crochet; **MB** = make bobble as follows: [K1, P1, K1, P1] all in next st, turn, P4, turn, K4, turn, [P2 tog] twice, turn, K2 tog; **ss** = slip stitch; **tr** = treble.
Also see page 5.

## NOTE
Read Charts from right to left on right side rows and from left to right on wrong side rows. When working motifs, use separate lengths of contrast yarns for each coloured area and twist yarns together on wrong side when changing colour to avoid holes.

## CARDIGAN

### BACK
With 4 mm (No 8/US 5) needles and MC, cast on 60 sts. Beg with a K row, work in st st and patt from Chart 1 until 76th row of Chart 1 has been worked.
**Shape Shoulders**
Cont in MC, cast off 10 sts at beg of next 2 rows and 9 sts at beg of foll 2 rows. Cast off rem 22 sts.

### LEFT FRONT
With 4 mm (No 8/US 5) needles and MC, cast on 29 sts.
Beg with a K row, work in st st and patt from Chart 1 until 50th row of Chart 1 has been worked.
**Shape Front**
Cont working from Chart 1, dec one st at front edge on next row and every foll 3rd row until 19 sts rem. Cont straight until 76th row of Chart 1 has been worked.
**Shape Shoulder**
Cont in MC, cast off 10 sts at beg of next row. Work 1 row. Cast off rem 9 sts.

### RIGHT FRONT
Work as given for Left Front, reversing shoulder shaping.

### SLEEVES
With 4 mm (No 8/US 5) needles and MC, cast on 30 sts.

Beg with a K row, work in st st and patt from Chart 1, inc one st at each end of 3rd row and every foll 4th row until there are 50 sts, working inc sts into patt. Cont straight until 48th row of Chart 1 has been worked. Cast off.

### TO MAKE UP
Join shoulder seams. Sew on sleeves, placing centre of sleeves to shoulder seams. Join side and sleeve seams.
**Crochet edging**
With crochet hook, MC, right side facing and beg at Right Front side seam, work 1 round of dc (the number of dc should be divisible by 3) along cast on edge of Right Front, up Right Front, across back neck, down Left Front, along cast on edge of Left Front and Back, working 3 dc in corners, ss in first dc.
**Next round** [2 tr in same dc as ss, miss 2 dc, ss in next dc] to end, making 4 buttonhole loops along straight edge of Right Front by working 3 ch, miss 2 dc, ss in next dc. Fasten off.
Work crochet edging along cast on edge of sleeves. Sew on buttons.
With Yellow, embroider cockerels' beaks and with Brown outline sheep with short straight stitches (see diagram page 56).

## BABY BLANKET

**BOBBLE MOTIF** – worked over 19 sts.
**1st row** (right side) K19.
**2nd row** P19.
**3rd and 4th rows** Work 1st and 2nd rows.
**5th row** K9, MB, K9.
**6th row** P19.
**7th and 8th rows** As 1st and 2nd rows.
**9th row** K6, MB, K5, MB, K6.
**10th to 12th rows** Work 6th to 8th rows.
**13th row** K3, MB, K11, MB, K3.
**14th to 20th rows** Work 6th to 12th rows.
**21st row** As 5th row.
**22nd row** P19.

### TO MAKE
With 4 mm (No 8/US 5) needles and MC, cast on 107 sts. K 4 rows.
Work in patt as follows:
**1st row** (right side) K2MC, K across 1st row of Chart 2, with MC, K2, work 1st row of bobble motif, K2, K across 1st row of Chart 3, with MC, K2, work 1st row of bobble motif, K2, K across 1st row of Chart 4, K2MC.
**2nd row** K2MC, P across 2nd row of Chart 4, with MC, K2, work 2nd row of bobble motif, K2, P across 2nd row of Chart 3, with MC, K2, work 2nd row of bobble motif, K2, P across 2nd row of Chart 2, K2MC.
**3rd to 22nd rows** Rep last 2 rows 10 times more, but working 3rd to 22nd rows of Charts and bobble motifs.
**23rd to 26th rows** With MC, K.
**27th row** With MC, K2, work 1st row of bobble motif, K2, K across 1st row of Chart 5, with MC, K2, work 1st row of bobble motif, K2, K across 1st row of Chart 2, with MC, K2, work 1st row of bobble motif, K2.
**28th row** With MC, K2, work 2nd row of bobble motif, K2, P across 2nd row of Chart 2, with MC, K2, work 2nd row of bobble motif, K2, P across 2nd row of Chart 5, with MC, K2, work 2nd row of bobble motif, K2.
**29th to 48th rows** Work 3rd to 22nd rows.
**49th to 52nd rows** With MC, K.
**53rd to 78th rows** Work 1st to 26th rows, but working Chart 6 instead of Chart 2, Chart 7 instead of Chart 3 and Chart 8 instead of Chart 4.
**79th to 104th rows** Work 27th to 52nd rows, but working Chart 4 instead of Chart 5 and Chart 3 instead of Chart 2.
**105th to 130th rows** Work 1st to 26th rows, but working Chart 9 instead of Chart 3 and Chart 7 instead of Chart 4.
**131st to 156th rows** Work 27th to 52nd rows, but working Chart 4 instead of Chart 2.
**157th to 182nd rows** Work 1st to 26th rows, but working Chart 6 instead of Chart 2, Chart 2 instead of Chart 3 and Chart 10 instead of Chart 4.

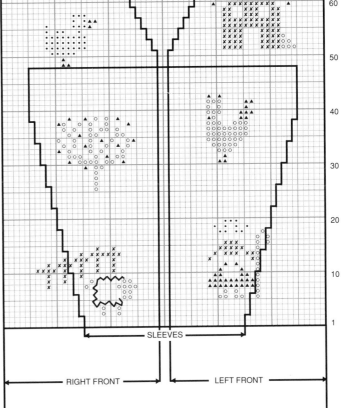

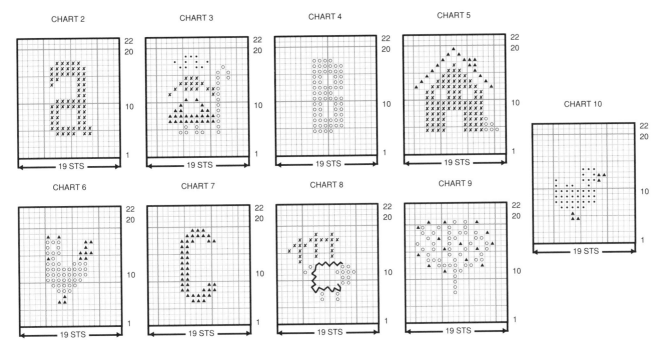

**183rd to 208th rows** Work 27th to 52nd rows, but working Chart 7 instead of Chart 5 and Chart 3 instead of Chart 2.
Cast off.
Work crochet edging around four sides as given for Cardigan. With Yellow, embroider cockerels' beaks and with Brown, outline sheep with short straight stitches (see diagram this page).

**CHART 1**

76
70
60
50
40
30
20
10
1

SLEEVES

RIGHT FRONT — LEFT FRONT

BACK

**KEY**

□ = Cream   ○ = Brown   ▲ = Red

x = Blue   • = Yellow

∿∿∿ = Short straight stitches

**CHART 2**

22
20
10
1
19 STS

**CHART 3**

22
20
10
1
19 STS

**CHART 4**

22
20
10
1
19 STS

**CHART 5**

22
20
10
1
19 STS

**CHART 10**

22
20
10
1
19 STS

**CHART 6**

22
20
10
1
19 STS

**CHART 7**

22
20
10
1
19 STS

**CHART 8**

22
20
10
1
19 STS

**CHART 9**

22
20
10
1
19 STS

# *Duck All-in-One*

See Page
7

### MEASUREMENTS

| To fit age | 0–3 | 3–6 | 6–9 | Months |
|---|---|---|---|---|
| Actual chest measurement | 53 | 56 | 59 | cm |
|  | 21 | 22 | 23¼ | in |
| Length from beginning of leg cuff to back neck | 44 | 48 | 52 | cm |
|  | 17½ | 19 | 20½ | in |
| Inside leg seam | 9 | 11 | 13 | cm |
|  | 3½ | 4¼ | 5 | in |
| Sleeve seam | 14 | 16 | 18 | cm |
|  | 5½ | 6¼ | 7 | in |

### MATERIALS
6(7:7) 50 g balls of Rowan Designer DK Wool in Cream (MC).
1(2:2) 50 g balls of same in Gold (A).
Oddment of Black for embroidery.
Pair each of 3¼ mm (No 10/US 3) and 4 mm (No 8/US 5) knitting needles.
6 buttons. Piece of thin foam.

### TENSION
24 sts and 32 rows to 10 cm/4 in square over st st on 4 mm (No 8/US 5) needles.

### ABBREVIATIONS
See page 5.

### LEFT FOOT
**Upper Foot** – knitted sideways.
With 4 mm (No 8/US 5) needles and A, cast on 20(21:22) sts.
Beg with a K row, work 10(12:14) rows in st st.
** Make tucks as follows:
**1st to 4th rows** Work 4 rows in st st.
**5th row** [K next st tog with corresponding st 4 rows below] to end.
**6th row** P.
**7th row** K17(18:19), turn.
**8th row and 3 foll alt rows** Sl 1, P to end.
**9th row** K14(15:15), turn.
**11th row** K11, turn.
**13th row** K7, turn.
**15th row** K3, turn.
**16th row** Sl 1, P to end.
Rep these 16 rows once more, then work 1st to 6th rows again. **
Work a further 38(42:46) rows in st st.
Cast off.
**Sole**
With right side of work facing, 4 mm (No 8/US 5) needles and A, pick up and K6(7:8) sts along lower (wider) edge of upper foot to centre of first tuck, [pick up and K10 sts to centre of next tuck] twice, pick up and K31(33:35) sts to cast off edge. 57(60:63) sts.
Beg with a P row, work 5 rows in st st.
**Next row** [K next st tog with corresponding st 5 rows below] to end.
**Dec row** P0(2:2), [P8(8:6), P2 tog] 3(3:4) times, [P2, P2 tog] 6(7:7) times, P3(0:1). 48(50:52) sts.
**Shape Sole**
**1st row** [K8(8:9), K2 tog tbl, K5, K2 tog, K7(8:8)] twice.
**2nd row and 2 foll alt rows** P.
**3rd row** [K8(8:9), K2 tog tbl, K3, K2 tog, K7(8:8)]twice.

**5th row** [K8(8:9), K2 tog tbl, K1, K2 tog, K7(8:8)] twice.
**7th row** [K8(8:9), sl 1, K2 tog, psso, K7(8:8)] twice.
Cast off purlwise.

### LEFT LEG
*** With right side of work facing, 3¼ mm (No 10/US 3) needles and MC, pick up and K43(45:47) sts along top edge of foot.
**1st row** K1, [P1, K1] to end.
**2nd row** P1, [K1, P1] to end.
Rep last 2 rows twice more.
**Inc row** [Rib 1, m1] 5 times, [rib 1, m1, rib 2, m1] to last 5(7:6) sts, [rib 1, m1] 4(5:5) times, rib 1(2:1). 74(77:81) sts.
Change to 4 mm (No 8/US 5) needles.
Beg with a K row, work in st st until Leg measures 9(11:13) cm/3½ (4¼:5) in from beg of rib, ending with a P row.
**Shape Crotch**
Cast off 3 sts at beg of next 2 rows. Dec one st at beg of next 4 rows. 64(67:71) sts. *** Leave these sts on a spare needle.

### RIGHT FOOT
**Upper Foot** – knitted sideways.
With 4 mm (No 8/US 5) needles and A, cast on 20(21:22) sts.
Beg with a K row, work 38(42:46) rows in st st.
Work as for Upper Foot of Right Foot from ** to **.
Work a further 10(12:14) rows in st st.
Cast off.
**Sole**
With right side of work facing, 4 mm (No 8/US 5) needles and A, pick up and K31(33:35) sts along lower (wider) edge of upper foot to centre of first tuck, [pick up and K10 sts to centre of next tuck]

twice, pick up and K6(7:8) sts to cast off edge. 57(60:63) sts.
Beg with a P row, work 5 rows in st st.
**Next row** [K next st tog with corresponding st 5 rows below] to end.
**Dec row** P3(0:1), [P2 tog, P2] 6(7:7) times, [P2 tog, P8(8:6)] 3(3:4) times, P0(2:2). 48(50:52) sts.
**Shape Sole**
**1st row** [K7(8:8), K2 tog tbl, K5, K2 tog, K8(8:9)] twice.
**2nd row and 2 foll alt rows** P.
**3rd row** [K7(8:8), K2 tog tbl, K3, K2 tog, K8(8:9)] twice.
**5th row** [K7(8:8), K2 tog tbl, K1, K2 tog, K8(8:9)] twice.
**7th row** [K7(8:8), sl 1, K2 tog, psso, K8(8:9)] twice.
Cast off purlwise.

### RIGHT LEG
Work as for Left Leg from *** to ***

### MAIN PART
**Next row** (right side) K across Right Leg sts then Left Leg sts.128(134:142) sts.
Work 13 rows straight.
**Shape Front Opening**
Cast off 3 sts at beg of next 2 rows. 122(128:136) sts.
Cont straight until work measures 30(33:36) cm/12(13:14¼) in from beg of rib, ending with a P row.
**Divide for Right Front**
**Next row** K29(31:33) sts, turn.
Work on this set of sts only. Cont in st st for a further 9(10:11) cm/3½ (4:4¼) in, ending at front edge.
**Shape Neck**
Cast off 3 sts at beg of next row. Dec one st at neck edge on every row until 21(22:23) sts rem. Cont straight until armhole measures 14(15:16) cm/5½(6:6¼) in, ending at armhole edge.
**Shape Shoulder**
Cast off 10(11:11) sts at beg of next row.
Work 1 row. Cast off rem 11(11:12) sts.
**Divide for Back**
With right side facing, rejoin yarn to rem sts and K64(66:70) sts, turn.
Work on this set of sts only. Cont in st st until Back matches Right Front to shoulder shaping, ending with a P row.
**Shape Shoulders**
Cast off 10(11:11) sts at beg of next 2 rows and 11(11:12) sts at beg of foll 2 rows. Leave rem 22(22:24) sts on a holder.
**Left Front**
With right side facing, rejoin yarn to rem sts and K to end. Complete to match Right Front.

### SLEEVES
With 3¼ mm (No 10/US 3) needles and MC, cast on 34(36:38) sts.
Work 3 cm/1¼ in in K1, P1 rib.
**Inc row** Rib 0(1:2), [inc in next st, rib 2] 11 times, inc in next st, rib 0(1:2).

46(48:50) sts.
Change to 4 mm (No 8/US 5) needles.
Beg with a K row, work in st st, inc one st
at each end of every 3rd row until there
are 66(70:76) sts. Cont straight until
Sleeve measures 14(16:18) cm/5½(6¼:7)
in from beg, ending with a P row. Cast off.

## NECKBAND AND HOOD
Join shoulder seams.
With right side of work facing, 3¼ mm (No
10/US 3) needles and MC, pick up and K
19(20:21) sts up right front neck, K across
back neck sts, inc one st at centre, pick
up and K19(20:21) sts down left front
neck. 61(63:67) sts.
**1st row** P1, [K1, P1] to end.
**2nd row** K1, [P1, K1] to end.
Rep last 2 rows twice more.
**Inc row** Rib 5 and slip these sts onto a
safety pin, rib 5(5:4), inc in next st, [rib
9(6:7), inc in next st] 4(6:6) times, rib
5(5:4), slip last 5 sts onto a safety pin.
56(60:64) sts.
Change to 4 mm (No 8/US 5) needles.
Beg with a K row, work in st st for
12(14:16) cm/4¾(5½:6¼) in for hood,
ending with a P row.
**Shape Top**
**Next row** K37(39:41) sts, K2 tog tbl, turn.

**Next row** Sl 1, P18, P2 tog, turn.
**Next row** Sl 1, K18, K2 tog tbl, turn.
Rep last 2 rows until all sts are worked off
on either side of centre sts.
Leave rem 20 sts on a holder.

## HOOD EDGING
With right side of work facing, 3¼ mm (No
10/US 3) needles and MC, rib across 5
sts from right side of hood, pick up and K
26(29:32) sts up right side of hood, K
across centre sts, dec one st, pick up and
K 26(29:32) sts down left side of hood,
then rib 5 sts from safety pin. 81(87:93)
sts. Rib 7 rows. Cast off in rib.

## BUTTONHOLE BAND
With right side of work facing, 3¼mm (No
10/US 3) needles and MC, pick up and
K 77(83:89) sts evenly along right side of
front opening to top of hood edging.
Work 3 rows in rib as on Neckband.
**1st buttonhole row** Rib 7(8:9), [cast off
2, rib 10(11:12) sts more] 5 times, cast off
2, rib to end.
**2nd buttonhole row** Rib to end, casting
on 2 sts over those cast off in previous
row.
Rib 4 rows. Cast off in rib.

## BUTTON BAND
Work to match Buttonhole Band omitting
buttonholes.

## BEAK (make 2)
With 4 mm (No 8/US 5) needles and A,
cast on 18 sts.
Beg with a P row, work in st st, inc one st
at each end of 2nd row and 2 foll rows. 24
sts. Work 15 rows straight. Cast off.

## TO MAKE UP
Join sole, foot and leg seams, then back
crotch seam. Join front crotch and centre
seam to front opening. Overlap
buttonhole band over button band and
catch down at base of opening. Sew in
sleeves, placing centre of sleeves to
shoulder seams. Join sleeve seams. With
right side of beak pieces together, join
seam all round beg and ending 3 cm/1¼
in from cast off edges. Turn to right side.
Cut a piece of foam to fit beak and place
inside. Place top open end of beak over
hood edging at centre and bottom end
and foam under the edging and slip stitch
in place. With Black, embroider eyes.
Sew on buttons.

# Cow All-in-One

See Page
8

| MEASUREMENTS To fit age | 0–3 | 3–6 | 6–9 | Months |
|---|---|---|---|---|
| Actual chest measurement | 53 | 56 | 59 | cm |
| | 21 | 22 | 23¼ | in |
| Length from beginning of leg cuff to centre back neck | 44 | 48 | 52 | cm |
| | 17¼ | 19 | 20½ | in |
| Inside leg seam | 9 | 11 | 13 | cm |
| | 3½ | 4¼ | 5 | in |
| Sleeve seam | 14 | 16 | 18 | cm |
| | 5½ | 6¼ | 7 | in |

## MATERIALS
5(6:6) 50 g balls of Rowan Designer
DK Wool in Cream (MC).
3(3:3) 50 g balls of same in Black (A).
Small amount of same in Brown.
Pair each of 3¼ mm (No 10/US 3) and
4 mm (No 8/US 5) knitting needles.
6 large and 4 small matching buttons.

## TENSION
22 sts and 44 rows to 10 cm/4 in
square over garter st (every row K) on
4 mm (No 8/US 5) needles.

## ABBREVIATIONS
See page 5.

## NOTE
Read Charts from right to left on right
side rows and from left to right on
wrong side rows. When working in
pattern, use separate small balls of
yarn for each coloured area and twist
yarns together on wrong side when
changing colour to avoid holes.

## LEFT FOOT
With 4 mm (No 8/US 5) needles and A,
cast on 32(34:36) sts.
**1st row and 4 foll alt rows (right side)**
K.

**2nd row** [K13(14:15), m1, K1, m1, K2]
twice.
**4th row** [K13(14:15), m1, K3, m1, K2]
twice.
**6th row** [K13(14:15), m1, K5, m1, K2]
twice.
**8th row** [K13(14:15), m1, K7, m1, K2]
twice.
**10th row** [K13(14:15), m1, K9, m1, K2]
twice. 52(54:56) sts.
**11th to 15th rows** K.
**16th row** K13(14:15), K2 tog tbl, K7, K2
tog, K to end.
**17th to 19th rows** K.
**20th row** K13(14:15), K2 tog tbl, K5, K2
tog, K to end.
**21st to 23rd rows** K.
**24th row** K13(14:15), K2 tog tbl, K3, K2
tog, K to end.
**25th row and 4 foll alt rows** K.
**26th row** K12(13:14), K2 tog, K3, K2 tog
tbl, K to end.
**28th row** K11(12:13), K2 tog, K3, K2 tog
tbl, K to end.
**30th row** K10(11:12), K2 tog, K3, K2 tog
tbl, K to end.
**32nd row** K9(10:11), K2 tog, K3, K2 tog
tbl, K to end.
**34th row** K8(9:10), K2 tog, K3, K2 tog
tbl, K to end. 36(38:40) sts.
**Left Leg**
** Change to MC and K 1 row.
Change to 3¼ mm (No 10/US 3) needles.
**Next row (wrong side)** *[K1, P1] twice,
[K1, P1] all in next st; rep from * to last
1(3:5) sts, [K1, P1] 0(1:2) times, K1.
43(45:47) sts.
**Next row** P1, [K1, P1] to end.
**Next row** K1, [P1, K1] to end.
Work a further 3 rows in rib.
**Next row** Rib 3(3:2), [m1, rib 1, m1, rib 2]
13(13:14) times, [m1, rib 2] 0(1:1) time,

rib 1. 69(72:76) sts.
Change to 4 mm (No 8/US 5) needles. **
Cont in garter st, work 8(16:24) rows.
Place Chart 1 as follows:
**Next row** (right side) K25(26:28)MC, K across 1st row of Chart 1, K25(27:29)MC.
**Next row** K25(27:29)MC, K across 2nd row of Chart 1, K25(26:28)MC.
Work a further 10 rows as set.
Place Chart 2 as follows:
**Next row** K11(12:14)MC, K across 1st row of Chart 2, patt to end.
**Next row** Patt to last 23(24:26) sts, K across 2nd row of Chart 2, K11(12:14)MC.
Work a further 14 rows as set.
**Shape Crotch**
Keeping patt correct, cast off 3 sts at beg of next 2 rows. Dec one st at beg of next 4 rows, working sts in MC when Chart 2 has been completed.
Leave rem 59(62:66) sts on a holder.

## RIGHT FOOT

With 4 mm (No 8/US 5) needles and A, cast on 32(34:36) sts.
**1st row and 4 foll alt rows** (right side) K.
**2nd row** [K2, m1, K1, m1, K13(14:15)] twice.
**4th row** [K2, m1, K3, m1, K13(14:15)] twice.
**6th row** [K2, m1, K5, m1, K13(14:15)] twice.
**8th row** [K2, m1, K7, m1, K13(14:15)] twice.
**10th row** [K2, m1, K9, m1, K13(14:15)] twice. 52(54:56) sts.
**11th to 15th rows** K.
**16th row** K28(29:30), K2 tog tbl, K7, K2 tog, K to end.
**17th to 19th rows** K.
**20th row** K28(29:30), K2 tog tbl, K5, K2 tog, K to end.
**21st to 23rd rows** K.
**24th row** K28(29:30), K2 tog tbl, K3, K2 tog, K to end.
**25th row and 4 foll alt rows** K.
**26th row** K27(28:29), K2 tog, K3, K2 tog tbl, K to end.
**28th row** K26(27:28), K2 tog, K3, K2 tog tbl, K to end.
**30th row** K25(26:27), K2 tog, K3, K2 tog tbl, K to end.
**32nd row** K24(25:26), K2 tog, K3, K2 tog tbl, K to end.
**34th row** K23(24:25), K2 tog, K3, K2 tog tbl, K to end. 36(38:40) sts.
**Right Leg**
Work as Left Leg from ** to **. Cont in garter st, work 16(24:32) rows.
Place Chart 3 as follows:
**Next row** (right side) K14(16:18)MC, K across 1st row of Chart 3, K19(20:22)MC.
**Next row** K19(20:22)MC, K across 2nd row of Chart 3, K14(16:18)MC.
Work a further 18 rows as set.
**Shape Crotch**
Cast off 3 sts at beg of next 2 rows. Dec one st at beg of next 4 rows. 59(62:66) sts.
**Body**
**Next row** Patt across Right Leg sts, then Left Leg sts. 118(124:132) sts.
Work a further 13 rows, working sts in MC when Chart 1 has been completed.

**Shape Front Opening**
Cast off 3 sts at beg of next 2 rows.
112(118:126) sts.
Patt 30(32:34) rows.
Place Chart 4 as follows:
**Next row** Patt to last 25(27:29) sts, K across 1st row of Chart 4, K5(7:9)MC.
**Next row** K5(7:9)MC, K across 2nd row of Chart 4, patt to end.
Work a further 18 rows as set.
Place Chart 5 as follows:
**Next row** Patt 54(56:58), K across 1st row of Chart 5, patt to end.
**Next row** Patt 34(38:44), K across 2nd row of Chart 5, patt to end.
Cont as set until work measures 30(33:36) cm/11¾(13:14) in from beg of rib, working sts in MC when Chart 3 has been completed and ending with a wrong side row.
**Right Front**
**Next row** K26(28:30), turn.
Work on this set of sts only. Cont straight for a further 9(10:11) cm/3½(4:4¼) in, ending with a wrong side row.
**Shape Neck**
Cast off 3 sts at beg of next row. Dec one st at neck edge on every row until 19(20:21) sts rem. Cont straight until work measures 44(48:52) cm/17¼(19:20½) in from beg of rib, ending with a right side row.
**Shape Shoulder**
Cast off 10(10:11) sts at beg of next row. K 1 row. Cast off rem 9(10:10) sts.
**Back**
With right side facing, rejoin yarn to rem sts and patt 60(62:66) sts, turn.
Work on this set of sts only. Cont straight until Back matches Right Front to shoulder shaping, working sts in MC when Chart 5 has been completed and ending with a wrong side row.
**Shape Shoulders**
Cast off 10(10:11) sts at beg of next 2 rows and 9(10:10) sts at beg of foll 2 rows. Leave rem 22(22:24) sts on a holder.
**Left Front**
With right side facing, rejoin yarn to rem 26(28:30) sts and patt to end.
Complete to match Right Front, working sts in MC when Chart 4 has been completed and reversing shapings.

## RIGHT MITTEN

*** With 4 mm (No 8/US 5) needles and A, cast on 16 sts.
**1st row and 2(3:3) foll alt rows** (wrong side) K.
**2nd row** [K1, m1, K6, m1, K1] twice.
**4th row** [K1, m1, K8, m1, K1] twice.
**6th row** [K1, m1, K10, m1, K1] twice.
**2nd and 3rd sizes only**
**8th row** [K1, m1, K12, m1, K1] twice.
**All sizes**
K 3 rows.
**Next row** K1, m1, K12(16:14), [m1, K2] 1(0:1) time, m1, K12(15:14), [m1, K1] 1(0:1) time. 32(34:36) sts.
K25(29:33) rows. Change to MC and K 1 row. ***
Change to 3¼ mm (No 10/US 3) needles.
**Next row** Cast on 8(9:9) sts, K0(0:1), [P1, K1] to last 0(1:0) st, P0(1:0).

**Next row** K0(1:0), [P1, K1] 8(8:9) times, turn.
Work on this set of sts only. **** Rib 1 row.
**1st buttonhole row** Rib 3, cast off 1, rib to last 4 sts, cast off 1, rib to end.
**2nd buttonhole row** Rib 3, cast on 1, rib to last 3 sts, cast on 1, rib 3.
Rib 2 rows. Cast off in rib. ****
**Right Sleeve**
With 3¼ mm (No 10/US 3) needles and right side facing, rejoin MC yarn to rem sts, cast on 8(8:9) sts, K0(0:1), [P1, K1] to last 0(0:1) st, P0(0:1). 32(34:36) sts.
Rib 4 rows.
**Next row** (wrong side) Rib 3(3:4), m1, [rib 5(4:3), m1] to last 4(3:5) sts, rib to end. 38(42:46) sts.
Change to 4 mm (No 8/US 5) needles.
Cont in garter st, work 10(14:18) rows, inc one st at each end of 3(3:4) foll 3rd (4th: 4th) rows. 44(48:54) sts.
Place Chart 6 as follows:
**Next row** K4(6:9)MC, K across 1st row of Chart 6, K15(17:20)MC.
**Next row** With MC, K twice in first st, K14(16:19), K across 2nd row of Chart 6, with MC, K3(5:8), K twice in last st.
Cont as set until Chart 6 has been completed, **at the same time**, inc one st at each end of every foll 3rd(4th:4th) row until there are 62(66:70) sts, working inc sts in MC.
Cont in MC only until Sleeve measures 14(16:18) cm/5½(6¼:7) in from beg of rib, ending with a wrong side row. Cast off.

## LEFT MITTEN

Work as given for Right Mitten from *** to ***.
Change to 3¼ mm (No 10/US 3) needles.
**Next row** P0(1:0), [K1, P1] 8(8:9) times, turn.
Work on this set of sts only.
**Next row** [K1, P1] to last 0(1:0) st, K0(1:0).
Work as given for Right Mitten from **** to ****.
**Left Sleeve**
With 3¼ mm (No 10/US 3) needles and wrong side facing, rejoin MC yarn to rem sts, cast on 8(9:9) sts, P0(1:1), [K1, P1] to last 0(1:0) st, K0(1:0).
**Next row** Cast on 8(8:9), P0(1:1), [K1, P1] to last 0(1:1) st, K0(1:1). 32(34:36) sts. Rib 4 rows.
**Next row** (wrong side) Rib 3(3:4), m1, [rib 5(4:3), m1] to last 4(3:5) sts, rib to end. 38(42:46) sts.
Change to 4 mm (No 8/US 5) needles.
Cont in garter st, work 4(6:10) rows, inc one st at each end of 1(1:2) foll 3rd (4th:4th) rows. 40(44:50) sts.
Place Chart 1 as follows:
**Next row** K20(22:25)MC, K across 1st row of Chart 1, K1(3:6)MC.
**Next row** With MC, K twice in first st, K0(2:4), K across 2nd row of Chart 1, with MC, K19(21:24), K twice in last st.
Complete to match Right Sleeve.

## NECKBAND

Join shoulder seams.
With 3¼ mm (No 10/US 3) needles, MC and right side facing, pick up and K 19(20:21) sts up right front neck, K across

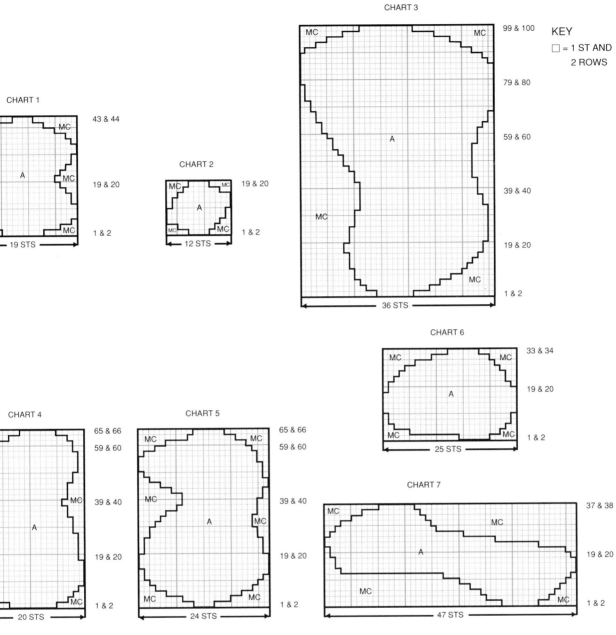

CHART 1

CHART 2

CHART 3

KEY
□ = 1 ST AND
2 ROWS

CHART 4

CHART 5

CHART 6

CHART 7

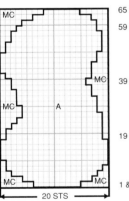

22(22:24) back neck sts, inc one st at centre, pick up and K 19(20:21) sts down left front neck. 61(63:67) sts.

**1st row** (wrong side) P1, [K1, P1] to end.

**2nd row** K1, [P1, K1] to end.
Rep last 2 rows twice more.

**Next row** Rib 5 and slip these sts onto a safety pin, rib 5(5:4), inc in next st, [rib 9(6:7), inc in next st] to last 10(10:9) sts, rib 5(5:4), slip last 5 sts onto a safety pin. 56(60:64) sts.

**Hood**
Change to 4 mm (No 8/US 5) needles.
Cont in garter st, work 8(12:16) rows.
Place Chart 7 as follows:

**Next row** K6(8:10)MC, K across 1st row of Chart 7, K3(5:7)MC.

**Next row** K3(5:7)MC, K across 2nd row of Chart 7, K6(8:10)MC.
Work a further 36 rows as set. Cont in MC

only until work measures 12(14:16) cm/4¾(5½:6¼) in from top of rib, ending with a wrong side row.

**Shape Top**

**Next row** K37(39:41), K2 tog, turn.

**Next row** K19, K2 tog tbl, turn.

**Next row** K19, K2 tog, turn.
Rep last 2 rows until all sts are worked off at each side of centre sts.
Leave rem 20 sts on a holder.

## HOOD EDGING

With 3¼ mm (No 10/US 3) needles, MC and right side facing, rib 5 sts from right side of hood safety pin, pick up and K 26(29:32) sts up right side of hood, K across 20 sts on holder, dec one st at centre, pick up and K 26(29:32) sts down left side of hood, rib 5 sts on left side safety pin. 81(87:93) sts.
Rib 7 rows. Cast off in rib.

## BUTTONHOLE BAND

With 3¼ mm (No 10/US 3) needles, MC and right side facing, pick up and K 77(83:89) sts evenly along right side edge of front opening to top of hood edging. Work 3 rows in rib as given for Neckband.

**1st buttonhole row** Rib 7(8:9), [cast off 2, rib 10(11:12) sts more] 5 times, cast off 2, rib to end.

**2nd buttonhole row** Rib to end, casting on 2 sts over those cast off in previous row.
Rib 4 rows. Cast off in rib.

## BUTTON BAND

Work to match Buttonhole Band omitting buttonholes.

## EARS (make 2)

With 4 mm (No 8/US 5) needles and A,

cast on 16 sts. Work 4 rows in garter st. Cont in garter st, dec one st at each end of next row and every foll alt row until 2 sts rem. K2 tog and fasten off.

### HORNS (make 2)
With 4 mm (No 8/US 5) needles and Brown, cast on 12 sts. Work 8 rows in garter st. Cont in garter st, dec one st at

each end of every row until 2 sts rem. K2 tog and fasten off.

### TO MAKE UP
Join foot and leg seams, then back crotch seam. Join front crotch and centre seam to front opening. Lap buttonhole band over button band and catch down to base of opening. Join side seams of mittens,

leaving buttonhole band free. Join sleeve seams. Sew in sleeves. Sew on large buttons to button band and small buttons to sleeve cuffs. Fold ears in half at cast on row and catch down. Sew in place. Fold horns in half lengthwise and join seams. Sew in place.

# Garter Stitch Jacket with Hat and Hens

See Page

9

### MEASUREMENTS

| To fit age | 6–9 | 9–12 | 12–18 | Months |
|---|---|---|---|---|
| Actual chest measurement | 58 | 62 | 65 | cm |
| | 22¾ | 24½ | 25½ | in |
| Length | 28 | 31 | 34 | cm |
| | 11 | 12¼ | 13½ | in |
| Sleeve seam | 16 | 18 | 20 | cm |
| (with cuff turned back) | 6¼ | 7 | 8 | in |

### MATERIALS
**Jacket**
4(5:5) 50 g balls of Rowan Designer DK Wool.
6 buttons.
**Hat**
1(1:2) 50 g balls of Rowan Designer DK Wool.
**Hens**
Small amount of DK yarn in Rust or Cream.

Oddment in Black for embroidery.
Oddments of Yellow and Red felt.
Wadding.
Pipe cleaners.
Pair of 4mm (No 8/US 5) knitting needles.
### TENSION
22 sts and 44 rows to 10 cm/4 in square over garter st (every row K).
### ABBREVIATIONS
See page 5.

### BACK
Cast on 64(68:72) sts. Work in garter st until Back measures 26(29:32) cm/ 10¼(11½:12¾) in from beg.
**Shape Neck**
*Next 2 rows K26(27:28), sl 1, yf, turn, sl 1, K to end.
Next 2 rows K23(24:25), sl 1, yf, turn, sl 1, K to end.
Next 2 rows K20(21:22), sl 1, yf, turn, sl 1, K to end.
Next row K to end. *
Rep from * to *. K 1 row. Cast off knitwise.

### POCKET LININGS (make 2)
Cast on 20(22:22) sts. Work 26(30:30) rows in garter st. Leave these sts on a holder.

### LEFT FRONT
Cast on 35(37:39) sts. Work 30(34:34) rows in garter st.
**Place Pocket**
Next row (wrong side) K9(9:10), cast off next 20(22:22) sts, K to end.
Next row K6(6:7), K across sts of pocket lining, K to end.
Cont in garter st across all sts until Front measures 25(28:31) cm/10(11:12¼) in from beg, ending at side edge.

**Shape Neck**
Next 2 rows K29(30:31), sl 1, yf, turn, sl 1, K to end.
Next 2 rows K27(28:29), sl 1, yf, turn, sl 1, K to end.
Next 2 rows K25(26:27), sl 1, yf, turn, sl 1, K to end.
Next 2 rows K23(24:25), sl 1, yf, turn, sl 1, K to end.
Next 2 rows K22(23:24), sl 1, yf, turn, sl 1, K to end.
Next 2 rows K21(22:23), sl 1, yf, turn, sl 1, K to end.
Next 2 rows K20(21:22), sl 1, yf, turn, sl 1, K to end.
Next row K to end. **
K 2 rows. Cast off knitwise. Mark front edge to indicate 6 buttons, first one 1 cm/½ in up from cast on edge and last one 1 cm/½ in down from cast off edge.

### RIGHT FRONT
Cast on 35(37:39) sts. Work 5 rows in garter st.
**1st buttonhole row** (right side) K2, cast off 2, K to end.
**2nd buttonhole row** K to last 2 sts, cast on 2, K2.
Work as given for Left Front to ** making buttonholes at markers and placing

pocket as follows:
Next row K6(6:7), cast off next 20(22:22) sts, K to end.
Next row K9(9:10), K across sts of pocket lining, K to end.
K 1 row. Cast off knitwise.

### SLEEVES
Cast on 41(43:45) sts. Work 42 rows in garter st. Cont in garter st, inc one st at each end of next row and every foll 6th row until there are 53(57:61) sts. Cont straight until Sleeve measures 21(23:25) cm/8¼(9:10) in from beg. Cast off.

### TO MAKE UP
Join shoulder seams. Sew on sleeves, placing centre of sleeves to shoulder seams. Join side and sleeve seams, reversing seams on cuffs. Turn back cuffs. Catch down pocket linings on wrong side. Sew on buttons.

### HAT
Cast on 81(89:97) sts. Cont in garter st until work measures 13(15:17) cm/ 5(6:6¾) in from beg.
**Shape Top**
Dec row K1, [K2 tog, K6] to end.
K 3 rows.
Dec row K1, [K2 tog, K5] to end.
K 1 row.
Dec row K1, [K2 tog, K4] to end.
Cont in this way, dec 10(11:12) sts at set on every alt row until 21(23:25) sts rem.
K 1 row.
Dec row K1, [K2 tog] to end.
Break off yarn, thread end through rem sts, pull up and secure. Join seam, reversing seam on last 4 cm/1¼ in for brim. Turn back brim.

### HENS
Cast on 20 sts. Work in garter st for 9 cm/3½ in. Cast off.
Fold diagonally and join one side to point. Stuff with wadding, then insert folded pipe cleaner in middle of wadding. Cut triangle in Yellow felt for beak and half circle in Red for wattle. Insert them into opening near top point, secure in position. Join opening. Cut 3 triangles along top edge of strip of Red felt for comb. Sew to top of head. With Black, embroider eyes. Form hen into shape. Make one more in same colour and one in another colour.

# Cow Cardigan

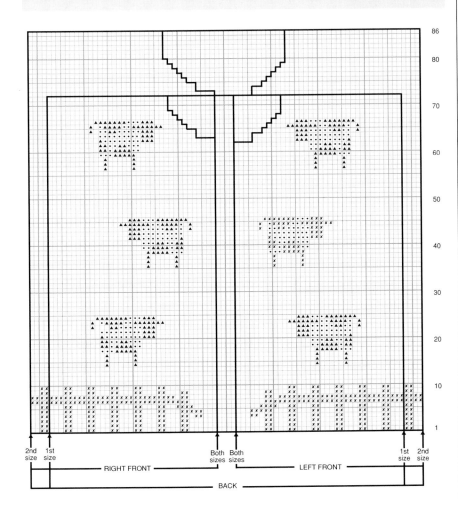

See Page
## 10

## MEASUREMENTS

| To fit age | 0–3 | 3–6 | Months |
|---|---|---|---|
| Actual chest measurement | 54 | 60 | cm |
| | 21¼ | 23½ | in |
| Length | 23 | 27 | cm |
| | 9 | 10½ | in |
| Sleeve seam | 14 | 17 | cm |
| | 5½ | 6¾ | in |

## MATERIALS
2(3) 50 g balls of Rowan Wool and Cotton in Green (MC).
1(1) 50 g ball of same in each of Brown, Black and Cream.
Pair each of 2¾ mm (No 12/US 1) and 3¼ mm (No 10/US 3) knitting needles.
7 buttons.

## TENSION
28 sts and 36 rows to 10 cm/4 in square over st st on 3¼ mm (No 10/US 3) needles.

## ABBREVIATIONS
See page 5.

## NOTE
Read Charts from right to left on right side rows and from left to right on wrong side rows. When working fence pattern, strand yarn not in use loosely across wrong side to keep fabric elastic. When working cow motifs, use separate lengths of contrast colours for each coloured area and twist yarns together on wrong side when changing colour to avoid holes.

## BACK
With 2¾ mm (No 12/US 1) needles and MC, cast on 75(83) sts.
**1st row** (right side) K1, [P1, K1] to end.
**2nd row** P1, [K1, P1] to end.
Rep last 2 rows until welt measures 3 cm/1¼ in from beg, ending with a wrong side row and inc one st at centre of last row. 76(84) sts.
Change to 3¼ mm (No 10/US 3) needles.
Beg with a K row, work in st st and patt from Chart 1 until 72nd(86th) row of Chart 1 has been worked.
### Shape Shoulders
With MC, cast off 13(14) sts at beg of next 2 rows and 13(15) sts at beg of foll 2 rows. Leave rem 24(26) sts on a holder.

## LEFT FRONT
With 2¾ mm (No 12/US 1) needles and MC, cast on 35(39) sts.
Work 3 cm/1¼ in in rib as given for Back welt, ending with a wrong side row and inc one st at centre of last row. 36(40) sts.
Change to 3¼ mm (No 10/US 3) needles.
Beg with a K row, work in st st and patt from Chart 1 until 61st(71st) row of Chart 1 has been worked.
### Shape Neck
Cont working from Chart 1, casting off 4 sts at beg of next row and 2 sts at beg of foll alt row. Dec one st at neck edge on every row until 26(29) sts rem. Patt 4(7) rows straight.
### Shape Shoulder
With MC, cast off 13(14) sts at beg of next row. Work 1 row. Cast off rem 13(15) sts.

## RIGHT FRONT
Work as given for Left Front, reversing shapings.

## SLEEVES
With 2¾ mm (No 12/US 1) needles and MC, cast on 37(39) sts. Work 3 cm/1¼ in in rib as given for Back welt, ending with a right side row.
**Inc row** Rib 1(3), [inc in next st, rib 3] 9 times. 46(48) sts.
Change to 3¼ mm (No 10/US 3) needles.
Beg with a K row, work in st st and patt from Chart 2 until 26th row of Chart 2 has been worked, **at the same time**, inc one st at each end of every foll 3rd row. 62(64) sts.
Cont in st st and MC only, inc one st at each end of next row and 0(2) foll 3rd rows. 64(70) sts. Cont straight until Sleeve measures 14(17) cm/5½(6¾) in from beg, ending with a P row. Cast off.

## NECKBAND
Join shoulder seams.
With 2¾ mm (No 12/US 1) needles, right side facing and MC, pick up and K 20(24) sts up right front neck, K across back neck sts, dec one st at centre, pick up and K 20(24) sts down left front neck. 63(73) sts. Beg with a 2nd row, work 9

rows in rib as given for Back welt. Cast off in rib.

## BUTTONHOLE BAND

With 2¾ mm (No 12/US 1) needles, right side facing and MC, pick up and K 63(69) sts evenly along front edge of Right Front to top of neckband.
Beg with a 2nd row, work 3 rows in rib as given for Back welt.
**1st buttonhole row** Rib 4, [cast off 2, rib 6(7) sts more] 6 times, cast off 2, rib to end.
**2nd buttonhole row** Rib to end, casting on 2 sts over those cast off in previous row.
Rib 4 rows. Cast off in rib.

## BUTTON BAND

Work to match Buttonhole Band, omitting buttonholes.

### KEY

□ = Green

✗ = Brown

▲ = Black

• = Cream

## TO MAKE UP

Sew on sleeves, placing centre of sleeves to shoulder seams. Join side and sleeve seams. Sew on buttons.

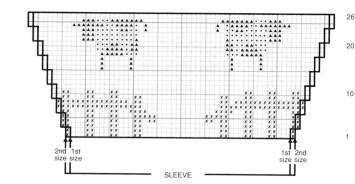

SLEEVE

# *Tartan Sweater with Chick*

See Page
*11*

## MEASUREMENTS

| To fit age | 6–12 | 12–18 | Months |
|---|---|---|---|
| Actual chest measurement | 69 | 75 | cm |
| | 27 | 29½ | in |
| Length | 29 | 32 | cm |
| | 11½ | 12½ | in |
| Sleeve seam | 19 | 22 | cm |
| | 7½ | 8½ | in |

## MATERIALS

3(4) 50 g balls of Rowan Cotton Glace in White (MC).
2(3) 50 g balls of same in Green (A).
1(1) 50 g ball of same in each of Navy (B) and Gold.
Small amount of same in Red.
Pair each of 2¾ mm (No 12/US 1) and 3¼ mm (No 10/US 3) knitting needles.
6 buttons.

## TENSION

26 sts and 32 rows to 10 cm/4 in square over check pattern on 3¼ mm (No 10/US 3) needles.

## ABBREVIATIONS

See page 5.

## NOTE

Read Chart from right to left on right side rows and from left to right on wrong side rows. When working check pattern, strand yarn not in use loosely across wrong side to keep fabric elastic. When working motif, use separate small balls of yarn for each coloured area and twist yarns together on wrong side when changing colour to avoid holes.

Cont in check patt until work measures 26(29) cm/10½ (11½) in from beg, ending with a wrong side row.
**Shape Neck**
**Next row** Patt 36(39), turn.
Work on this set of sts only. Keeping patt correct, dec one st at neck edge on next 5 rows. 31(34) sts. Cast off.
With right side facing, slip centre 18(20) sts onto a holder, rejoin yarn to rem sts and patt to end. Complete to match first side.

## FRONT

Work as given for Back to **.
Place motif as follows:
**Next row** Patt 25(29), K across 1st row of Chart, patt 25(29).
**Next row** Patt 25(29), P across 2nd row of Chart, patt 25(29).
Cont working as set until 33rd row of Chart has been worked.
Work in check patt across all sts until Front measures 24(27) cm/9¾(10¾) in from beg, ending with a wrong side row.
**Shape Neck**
**Next row** Patt 36(39), turn.
Work on this set of sts only. Dec one st at neck edge on every row until 31(34) sts rem. Cont straight until Front matches Back to cast off edge, ending with a wrong side row. Cast off.
With right side facing, slip centre 18(20) sts onto a holder, rejoin yarn to rem sts and patt to end. Complete to match first side.

## SLEEVES

With 2¾ mm (No 12/US 1) needles and MC, cast on 37(41) sts. Work 3 cm/1¼ in in rib as given for Back welt, ending with a right side row.
**Inc row** Rib 7(5), [inc in next st, rib 5(3)] to end. 42(50) sts.
Change to 3¼ mm (No 10/US 3) needles.
Work in check patt as given for Back, inc

## BACK

With 2¾ mm (No 12/US 1) needles and MC, cast on 83(91) sts.
**1st row** (right side) K1, [P1, K1] to end.
**2nd row** P1, [K1, P1] to end.
Rep last 2 rows until work measures 3 cm/1¼ in from beg, ending with a right side row.
**Inc row** Rib 8(6), inc in next st, [rib 10(12), inc in next st] 6 times, rib 8(6). 90(98) sts.
Change to 3¼ mm (No 10/US 3) needles. Work in check patt as follows:
**1st row** (right side) K5(3)MC, 2A, [4MC, 2A] to last 5(3) sts, 5(3)MC.

**2nd row** P in B.
**3rd row** As 1st row.
**4th row** P5(3)MC, 2A, [4MC, 2A] to last 5(3) sts, 5(3)MC.
**5th row** As 1st row.
**6th row** P in A.
**7th row** K in A.
**8th row** As 4th row.
**9th row** K in B.
**10th row** As 4th row.
**11th row** As 1st row.
**12th row** As 4th row.
**13th row** K in A.
**14th row** P in A.
These 14 rows form check patt. **

one st at each end of every foll 3rd(4th) row until there are 70(78) sts, working inc sts into patt.
Cont straight for a few rows until Sleeve measures 19(22) cm/7½(8½) in from beg, ending with a wrong side row. Cast off.

## BACK NECKBAND
With 2¾ mm (No 12/US 1) needles, MC and right side facing, pick up and K 6 sts down right back neck, K across centre back sts, dec one st, pick up and K 6 sts up left back neck. 29(31) sts. Beg with a 2nd row, work 7 rows in rib as given for Back welt. Cast off in rib.

## FRONT NECKBAND
With 2¾ mm (No 12/US 1) needles, MC and right side facing, pick up and K 14 sts down left front neck, K across centre front sts, dec one st, pick up and K 14 sts up right front neck. 45(47) sts. Complete as given for Back Neckband.

## BUTTONHOLE BANDS
With 2¾ mm (No 12/US 1) needles, MC and right side facing, pick up and K 35(37) sts along left front shoulder and row ends of neckband. Beg with a 2nd row, work 3 rows in rib as given for Back welt.
**1st buttonhole row** Rib 5, [cast off 2, rib until there are 10(11) sts] twice, cast off 2, rib until there are 4 sts.
**2nd buttonhole row** Rib to end, casting on 2 sts over those cast off in previous row.

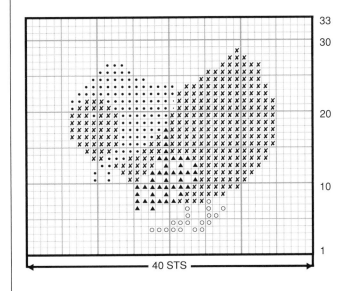

**33**
**30**
**20**
**10**
**1**

← 40 STS →

**KEY**
□ = White
▲ = Green
• = Navy
× = Gold
○ = Red

Rib 3 rows. Cast off in rib.
Work right front shoulder to match reversing buttonhole row.

## BUTTON BANDS
With 2¾ mm (No 12/US 1) needles, MC and right side facing, pick up and K 35(37) sts along right back shoulder and row ends of neckband. Beg with a 2nd row, work 8 rows in rib as given for Back

welt. Cast off in rib.
Work left back shoulder to match.

## TO MAKE UP
Lap buttonhole bands over button bands and catch down at side edges. Sew on sleeves, placing centre of sleeves in line with buttonholes. Join side and sleeve seams. Sew on buttons. With Red, embroider beak.

# *Farm Animals Slippers*

See Page
**12**

## MEASUREMENTS

| Duck and Rabbit | | |
| --- | --- | --- |
| To fit age | 0–6 | Months |
| **Pig** | | |
| To fit age | 6–12 | Months |

## MATERIALS
**Duck** 1 × 50 g ball of Rowan Designer DK Wool in each of Cream (A) and Orange (B).
Oddment of Black for embroidery.
Pair each of 3 mm (No 11/US 2) and 3¼ mm (No 10/US 3) knitting needles.
**Rabbit** 1 × 50 g ball of Rowan Designer DK Wool in each of Brown (A) and Pink (B).
Oddments of Black and Cream.
Pair each of 2¾ mm (No 12/US 1),

3 mm (No 11/US 2) and 3¼ mm (No 10/US 3) knitting needles.
**Pig** 2 × 50 g balls of Rowan DK Handknit Cotton in Pink.
Oddment of Black for embroidery.
Pair of 3 mm (No 11/US 2) knitting needles.

## ABBREVIATIONS
See page 5.

## DUCK

### MAIN PART
With 3 mm (No 11/US 2) needles and A, cast on 24 sts. K 40 rows. Cast off.
Make one more square in A and one in B. Place B square on one A square and join them together. With A side on the outside, fold 3 corners of square into centre forming an open envelope.
Join the 2 seams. Fold rem A square diagonally to form triangle and join edges. Place joined edges of triangle to edges of open end of envelope, matching points. Sew in place.

### BEAK
With 3¼ mm (No 10/US 3) needles and B, cast on 14 sts. Dec one st at each end of next row and 2 foll alt rows. K 1 row. Cast off. Make one more. Place pieces together and stitch all round, leaving cast on edges free. Turn to right side and join together cast on edges. Sew to front of main part. With Black, embroider eyes.
Make one more.

## RABBIT

### MAIN PART
Work as given for Main Part of Duck.

### OUTER EARS
With 3 mm (No 11/US 2) needles and A, cast on 7 sts. K 17 rows. Dec one st at each end of next row and foll 5th row. K 4 rows. K3 tog and fasten off. Make one more.

### INNER EARS
With 2¾ mm (No 12/US 1) needles and B, cast on 7 sts. K 17 rows. Dec one st at each end of next row and foll 5th row. K 2 rows. K3 tog and fasten off. Make one more.
Sew inner ears to outer ears. Fold cast on edges in half and stitch together along cast on edges and along first 1.5 cm/½ in. Sew in place.

### NOSE
With 3¼ mm (No 10/US 3) needles and Black, cast on one st.
**Next row** K into front, back, front, back and front of st.
**Next row** (right side) K.
**Next row** P.
**Next row** K2 tog, K1, K2 tog.
**Next row** P3 tog and fasten off.
Run a gathering thread around edges, pull up and secure. Attach to front of main part.
With Black, embroider eyes. With Cream, make a small pompon and attach to back of main part.
Make one more.

## PIG

### MAIN PART
Work as given for Main Part of Duck, but using one colour throughout.

### NOSE
With 3 mm (No 11/US 2) needles, cast on 4 sts. K 1 row. Inc one st at each end of next row and 2 foll alt rows, then at each end of foll row. 12 sts. K 6 rows. Dec one st at each end of next 2 rows then on 2 foll alt rows. K 1 row. Cast off. Make one more. Place pieces together and stitch all round, leaving cast on edges free. Turn to right side and join together cast on edges. Sew to front of main part. With Black, embroider nostrils.

### EARS
With 3 mm (No 11/US 2) needles, cast on 8 sts. K 2 rows. Dec one st at each end of next row and 2 foll alt rows. K2 tog and fasten off. Make one more. Sew in place.

### TAIL
With 3 mm (No 11/US 2) needles, cast on 14 sts. Cast off. Sew to back of main part. Make one more.

# *Sailor Collared Sweater with Duck Motifs*

See Page 14

## MEASUREMENTS

| To fit age | 3–6 | 6–12 | Months |
|---|---|---|---|
| Actual chest measurement | 56 | 61 | cm |
| | 22 | 24 | in |
| Length | 30 | 32 | cm |
| | 11¾ | 12½ | in |
| Sleeve seam | 16 | 18 | cm |
| | 6¼ | 7 | in |

### MATERIALS
5(5) 50 g balls of Rowan Cotton Glace in Navy (MC).
1(1) 50 g ball of same in White (A).
Small amount of same in each of Yellow (B) and Green (C).
Pair each of 2¼ mm (No 13/US 0) and 3 mm (No 11/US 2) knitting needles.

### TENSION
28 sts and 34 rows to 10 cm/4 in square over st st on 3 mm (No 11/US 2) needles.

### ABBREVIATIONS
See page 5.

### NOTE
Read Charts from right to left on right side rows and from left to right on wrong side rows. When working in pattern, use separate lengths of A, B and C yarn for each coloured area and twist yarns together on wrong side when changing colour to avoid holes.

### BACK
With 2¼ mm (No 13/US 0) needles and MC, cast on 79(85) sts. K 7 rows.
Change to 3 mm (No 11/US 2) needles.
**Next row** (right side) K.
**Next row** K3, P to last 3 sts, K3.
Rep last 2 rows twice more. Mark each end of last row. Beg with a K row, cont in st st, work 2 rows.
Place Charts as follows:
**Next row** [K5MC, K across 1st row of Chart 1] 3 times, K6MC, K across 1st row of Chart 2, K14(20)MC.
**Next row** P14(20)MC, P across 2nd row of Chart 2, P6MC, [P across 2nd row of Chart 1, P5MC] 3 times.
Cont in patt as set, work a further 20 rows, working sts in MC when all Chart 1 have been completed. Cont in MC across all sts until work measures 30(32) cm/11¾(12½) in from beg, ending with a P row.
Shape Shoulders and Neck
**Next row** Cast off 13(14) sts, K16(17) sts more, cast off next 19(21) sts, K to end.
Work on last set of sts only. Cast off 13(14) sts at beg of next row, 4 sts at beg of foll row. Cast off rem 13(14) sts.
With wrong side facing, rejoin yarn to rem sts, cast off 4 sts, p to end.
Cast off rem 13(14) sts.

### FRONT
Work as given for Back until Front measures 18(19) cm/7(7½) in from beg, ending with a P row.

Shape Neck
**Next row** K39(42), turn.
Work on this set of sts only. Dec one st at neck edge on 7 foll alt rows, then on every foll 3rd row until 26(28) sts rem. Cont straight until Front matches Back to shoulder shaping, ending at side edge.
Shape Shoulder
Cast off 13(14) sts at beg of next row. Work 1 row. Cast off rem 13(14) sts.
With right side facing, rejoin yarn to rem sts, cast off centre one st, K to end. Complete to match first side.

### SLEEVES
With 2¼ mm (No 13/US 0) needles and MC, cast on 45(47) sts. K 7 rows.
Change to 3 mm (No 11/US 2) needles.
Beg with a K row, work in st st inc one st at each end of 3rd(5th) row and every foll 4th row until there are 61(67) sts. Cont straight until Sleeve measures 16(18) cm/6¼(7) in from beg, ending with a P row. Cast off.

### COLLAR
With 2¼ mm (No 13/US 0) needles and MC, cast on 66(72) sts. K 7 rows, inc 3 sts evenly across last row. 69(75) sts.
Change to 3 mm (No 11/US 2) needles.
**Next row** (right side) K.
**Next row** K3, P to last 3 sts, K3.
Rep last 2 rows until Collar measures 12(14) cm/4¾(5½) in from beg, ending with a wrong side row.
Shape Neck
**Next row** K30(32), cast off next 9(11) sts, K to end.

Cont on last set of sts only for left side of front collar. Work 1 row.
Cast off 3 sts at beg of next row and 2 foll alt rows. Dec one st at inside edge on 3 foll 4th rows, 2 foll 3rd rows then on every foll alt row until 3 sts rem. Dec one st at inside edge on next 2 rows. Fasten off.
With wrong side facing, rejoin yarn to rem sts for right side of front collar and complete to match left side.

## INSET

With 3 mm (No 11/US 2) needles and A, cast on 3 sts.
Beg with a K row, work in st st and stripe

### CHART 2

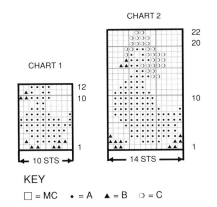

### KEY

□ = MC  • = A  ▲ = B  ○ = C

patt of 2 rows A and 2 rows MC, inc one st at each end of 2nd row and foll row, then on every alt row until there are 27(31) sts, ending with a P row. Cont in A only.
Change to 2¼ mm (No 13/US 0) needles.
**Next row** K4, K2 tog, [K7(5), K2 tog] to last 3(4) sts, K3(4). 24(27) sts.
K 4 rows. Cast off knitwise.

## TO MAKE UP

Sew on sleeves, placing centre of sleeves to shoulder seams. Beginning at markers, join side and sleeve seams. Sew on collar. Sew in inset. Wind C yarn round neck of each duck and tie into a bow.

# Sheep Waistcoat

See Page
15

| MEASUREMENTS To fit age | 12 | 18 | 24 | Months |
|---|---|---|---|---|
| Actual chest measurement | 53 | 56 | 59 | cm |
|  | 21 | 22 | 23¼ | in |
| Length | 27 | 29 | 31 | cm |
|  | 10½ | 11½ | 12 | in |

## MATERIALS

3(3:4) 25 g hanks of Rowan Donegal Lambswool in Charcoal (MC).
Small amount of same in each of Black and White.
Pair each of 2¾ mm (No 12/US 1) and 3¼ mm (No 10/US 3) knitting needles.
4 buttons.

## TENSION

28 sts and 40 rows to 10 cm/4 in square over st st on 3¼ mm (No 10/US 3) needles.

## ABBREVIATIONS

See page 5.

## NOTE

Read Chart from right to left on right side rows and from left to right on wrong side rows. When working motif, use separate lengths of contrast yarns for each coloured area and twist yarns together on wrong side when changing colour to avoid holes.

## BACK

With 2¾ mm (No 12/US 1) needles and MC, cast on 75(79:83) sts.
**1st row** (right side) K1, [P1, K1] to end.
**2nd row** P1, [K1, P1] to end.
Rep last 2 rows until work measures 2 cm/¾ in from beg, ending with a wrong side row.
Change to 3¼ mm (No 10/US 3) needles.
Beg with a K row, work in st st until Back measures 16(17:18) cm/6¼(6¾:7) in from beg, ending with a P row.
**Shape Armholes**
Cast off 5 sts at beg of next 2 rows. Dec one st at each end of next 3 rows, then on every foll alt row until 53(57:61) sts rem.
Cont straight until armholes measure 11(12:13) cm/4¼(4¾:5) in, ending with a K row.
**Shape Neck and Shoulders**
**Next row** P15(16:17), cast off next 23(25:27) sts, P to end.
Work on last set of sts only. Cast off 6(6:7) sts at beg of next row and 3 sts at beg of foll row. Cast off rem 6(7:7) sts.

With right side facing, rejoin yarn to rem sts, K to end. Cast off 6(6:7) sts at beg of next row and 3 sts at beg of foll row. Cast off rem 6(7:7) sts.

## LEFT FRONT

With 3¼ mm (No 10/US 3) needles and MC, cast on 2 sts. P 1 row.
Cont in st st, casting on 3 sts at beg of next row and 5 foll alt rows, **at the same time**, inc one st at end of next row and at same edge on foll 11 rows.
**2nd and 3rd sizes only**
Cast on (2:4) sts at beg of next row.
**All sizes**
32(34:36) sts. Cont straight until work measures 14(15:16) cm/5½(6:6¼) in from last set of cast on sts, ending with a P row.
**Shape Armhole and Neck**
**Next row** Cast off 5, K to last 2 sts, K2 tog.
Dec one st at neck edge on every foll 4th row, **at the same time**, dec one st at armhole edge on next 3 rows, then on 3 foll alt rows.

Keeping armhole edge straight, cont to dec at neck edge as before until 12 (13:14) sts rem. Cont straight until armhole measures 11(12:13) cm/4¼(4¾:5) in, ending with a P row.
**Shape Shoulder**
Cast off 6(6:7) sts at beg of next row.
Work 1 row. Cast off rem 6(7:7) sts.

## RIGHT FRONT

With 3¼ mm (No 10/US 3) needles and MC, cast on 2 sts. K 1 row.
Cont in st st, casting on 3 sts at beg of next row and 5 foll alt rows, **at the same time**, inc one st at end of next row and at same edge on foll 11 rows.
**2nd and 3rd sizes only**
Cast on (2:4) sts at beg of next row.
**All sizes**
32(34:36) sts. Work 1(0:0) row.
**Place Motif**
**Next row** K8(9:10)MC, K across 1st row of Chart, K14(15:16)MC.
**Next row** P14(15:16)MC, P across 2nd row of Chart, P8(9:10)MC.
Work a further 5 rows as set.
Cont in MC across all sts and complete as given for Left Front, reversing shapings.

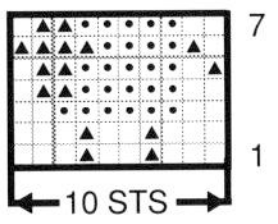

### KEY

□ = Charcoal
▲ = Black
• = White

## BUTTON BAND AND LAPEL

With 2¾ mm (No 12/US 1) needles and MC, cast on 10 sts. Work in P1, K1 rib until band when slightly stretched, fits lower edge of Left Front to point.
***Next 2 rows** Rib 7, yb, sl 1, yf, turn, sl 1, rib to end.
**Next 2 rows** Rib 5, yb, sl 1, yf, turn, sl 1, rib to end.
**Next 2 rows** Rib 3, yb, sl 1, yf, turn, sl 1, rib to end.
Rib 2 rows.

**Next 2 rows** Rib 3, yb, sl 1, yf, turn, sl 1, rib to end.
**Next 2 rows** Rib 5, yb, sl 1, yf, turn, sl 1, rib to end.
**Next 2 rows** Rib 7, yb, sl 1, yf, turn, sl 1, rib to end.*
Cont in rib across all sts until band when slightly stretched, fits lower edge of Left Front from point to corner, ending at outside edge.
Rep from * to *. Cont in rib across all sts until band fits along straight edge of Left Front to beg of neck shaping, ending at inside edge.
**Shape Lapel**
Inc one st at beg of next row and every foll alt row until there are 21 sts then on 1(2:3) foll 4th rows. 22(23:24) sts. Rib 2 rows. Cast off in rib. Sew in place, sewing lapel half way up neck shaping.
Mark position for 4 buttons along front edge of band, first one 2 rows after corner shaping and last one 2 rows below lapel shaping and rem 2 evenly spaced between.

## BUTTONHOLE BAND AND LAPEL
With 2¾ mm (No 12/US 1) needles and MC, cast on 10 sts. Work in K1, P1 rib until band when slightly stretched, fits along lower edge of Right Front to point.
*Next 2 rows** Rib 7, yf, sl 1, yb, turn, sl 1, rib to end.
**Next 2 rows** Rib 5, yf, sl 1, yb, turn, sl 1, rib to end.
**Next 2 rows** Rib 3, yf, sl 1, yb, turn, sl 1, rib to end.
Rib 2 rows.
**Next 2 rows** Rib 3, yf, sl 1, yb, turn, sl 1, rib to end.
**Next 2 rows** Rib 5, yf, sl 1, yb, turn, sl 1, rib to end.
**Next 2 rows** Rib 7, yf, sl 1, yb, turn, sl 1, rib to end.*
Complete as given for Button Band and Lapel, making buttonholes at markers as follows:
**1st buttonhole row** Rib 4, cast off 2, rib to end.
**2nd buttonhole row** Rib 4, cast on 2, rib to end.
Sew in place, sewing lapel half way up neck shaping.

## COLLAR
Join shoulder seams.
With 2¾ mm (No 12/US 1) needles, MC and right side facing, pick up and K 25 sts up rem right front neck, 5 sts down right back neck, 23(25:27) sts across back neck, 5 sts up left back neck and 25 sts down rem left front neck. 83(85:87) sts. Work in rib as given for Back welt for 5(5:6) cm/2(2:2¼) in. Cast off loosely in rib.

## ARMBANDS
With 2¾ mm (No 12/US 1) needles, MC and right side facing, pick up and K 75(83:91) sts evenly around armhole edge. Work 8 rows in rib as given for Back welt. Cast off in rib.

## TO MAKE UP
Join side and armband seams. Join collar and lapel for 2.5 cm/1 in from pick up row. Sew on buttons.

# *Aran Sweater with Farmyard Panel*

See Page 16

## MEASUREMENTS

| To fit age | 2 | Years |
|---|---|---|
| Actual chest measurement | 76 | cm |
| | 30 | in |
| Length | 41 | cm |
| | 16 | in |
| Sleeve seam | 25 | cm |
| | 10 | in |

## MATERIALS
9×50 g balls of Rowan DK Handknit Cotton in Brown (MC).
1×50 g ball of same in each of Red, Cream, Black, Yellow and Blue.
Pair each of 3¼ mm (No 10/US 3) and 4 mm (No 8/US 5) knitting needles.
Cable needle.

## TENSION
20 sts and 28 rows to 10 cm/4 in square over st st on 4 mm (No 8/US 5) needles.

## ABBREVIATIONS
C2B = slip next st onto cable needle and leave at back of work, K1, then K1 from cable needle;
C2F = slip next st onto cable needle and leave at front of work, K1, then K1 from cable needle;
Cr2L = slip next st onto cable needle and leave at front of work, P1, then K1 from cable needle;
Cr2R = slip next st onto cable needle and leave at back of work, K1, then P1 from cable needle;
MB = make bobble, [K1, P1, K1, P1] all in next st, turn, P4, turn, K4, turn, [P2 tog] twice, turn, K2 tog.
Also see page 5.

## NOTE
Read Chart from right to left on right side rows and from left to right on wrong side rows. When working motifs, use separate lengths of contrast yarn for each coloured area and twist yarns together on wrong side when changing colour to avoid holes.

## PANEL – worked over 18 sts.
**1st row** (wrong side) K8, P2, K8.
**2nd row** P7, C2B, C2F, P7.
**3rd row** K6, Cr2L, P2, Cr2R, K6.
**4th row** P5, Cr2R, C2B, C2F, Cr2L, P5.
**5th row** K4, Cr2L, K1, P4, K1, Cr2R, K4.
**6th row** P3, Cr2R, P1, Cr2R, K2, Cr2L, P1, Cr2L, P3.
**7th row** K3, P1, K2, P1, K1, P2, K1, P1, K2, P1, K3.
**8th row** P3, MB, P1, Cr2R, P1, K2, P1, Cr2L, P1, MB, P3.
**9th row** K5, P1, K2, P2, K2, P1, K5.
**10th row** P5, MB, P2, K2, P2, MB, P5.
These 10 rows form patt.

## BACK
With 3¼ mm (No 10/US 3) needles and MC, cast on 74 sts.
**1st row** (wrong side) K2, [P2, K2] to end.
**2nd row** P2, [K2, P2] to end.
Rep last 2 rows until work measures 4 cm/1½ in from beg, ending with a wrong side row.
**Inc row** Rib 3, [m1, rib 5] 3 times, rib 5, m1, rib 9, [m1, rib 3] 4 times, rib 7, m1, rib 5, [rib 5, m1] 3 times, rib 3. 86 sts.
Change to 4 mm (No 8/US 5) needles. Work in patt as follows:
**1st row** (wrong side) With MC, K1, work 1st row of Panel, [P across 1st row of Chart, with MC, work 1st row of Panel] twice, K1MC.

**2nd row** With MC, P1, work 2nd row of Panel, [K across 2nd row of Chart, with MC, work 2nd row of Panel] twice, P1MC. These 2 rows set position of Panels and Charts. Cont in patt as set until work measures 41 cm/16 in from beg, ending with a wrong side row.

**Shape Shoulders**
Cast off 13 sts at beg of next 2 rows and 14 sts at beg of foll 2 rows.
Leave rem 32 sts on a holder.

### FRONT
Work as given for Back until Front measures 35 cm/13¾ in from beg, ending with a wrong side row.

**Shape Neck**
**Next row** Patt 35, turn.
Work on this set of sts only. Keeping patt correct, dec one st at neck edge on every row until 27 sts rem. Cont straight until Front matches Back to shoulder shaping, ending at side edge.

**Shape Shoulder**
Cast off 13 sts at beg of next row. Patt 1 row. Cast off rem 14 sts.
With right side facing, slip centre 16 sts onto a holder, rejoin yarn to rem sts and patt to end. Complete to match first side.

### SLEEVES
With 3¼ mm (No 10/US 3) needles and MC, cast on 42 sts. Work 3 cm/1¼ in in rib as given for Back welt, ending with a wrong side row.
**Inc row** Rib 1, [m1, rib 5] to last st, m1, rib 1. 51 sts.
Change to 4 mm (No 8/US 5) needles.

Work in patt as follows:
**1st row** (wrong side) With MC, work 1st row of Panel, P across 1st row of Chart, with MC, work 1st row of Panel.
**2nd row** With MC, work 2nd row of Panel, K across 2nd row of Chart, with MC, work 2nd row of Panel.
These 2 rows set position of Panels and Chart. Cont in patt as set, inc one st at each end of next row and 8 foll 3rd rows, then on every foll 4th row until there are 79 sts, working inc sts into patt from Chart.
Cont straight until Sleeve measures 25 cm/10 in from beg, ending with a wrong side row. Cast off.

### NECKBAND
Join right shoulder seam.
With 3¼ mm (No 10/US 3) needles, MC and right side facing, pick up and K 17 sts down left front neck, K centre front sts, pick up and K 17 sts up right front neck, K back neck sts. 82 sts.
Beg with a 1st row, work 11 rows in rib as given for Back welt. Beg with a K row, work 5 rows in st st. Cast off purlwise.

### TO MAKE UP
Join left shoulder and neckband seam, reversing seam on st st section of neckband. Allow top of neckband to roll back. Sew on sleeves, placing centre of sleeves to shoulder seams. Join side and sleeve seams. With Black, embroider eyes and legs on chicks and eyes on ducklings.

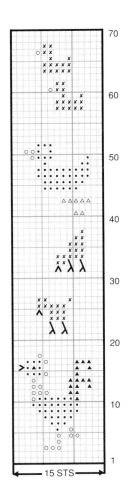

**KEY**
☐ = Brown
○ = Red
• = Cream
▲ = Black
× = Yellow
△ = Blue

λ ʌ = embroidery stitches

# Cotton Smock

See Page 17

## MEASUREMENTS

| To fit age | 2–3 | 3–4 | Years |
|---|---|---|---|
| Actual chest measurement | 69 | 77 | cm |
|  | 27 | 30¼ | in |
| Length | 50 | 56 | cm |
|  | 19¾ | 22 | in |
| Sleeve seam | 22 | 25 | cm |
|  | 8¾ | 10 | in |

### MATERIALS
11(13) 50 g balls of Rowan Cotton Glace.
Pair each of 2¼ mm (No 13/US 0) and 3 mm (No 11/US 2) knitting needles.
Cable needle.
6 buttons.

### TENSION
28 sts and 34 rows to 10 cm/4 in square over st st on 3 mm (No 11/US 2) needles.

### ABBREVIATIONS
**Cr2L** = sl next st onto cable needle and leave at front of work, P1, then K1 from cable needle;
**Cr2R** = sl next st onto cable needle and leave at back of work, K1, then P1 from cable needle;
**C2B** = sl next st onto cable needle and leave at back of work, K1, then K1 from cable needle;
**C2F** = sl next stitch onto cable needle and leave at front of work, then K1, from cable needle.
Also see page 5.

### PATTERN A
Rep of 8 sts.
**1st row** (right side) [P3, C2F, P3] to end.
**2nd row** [K2, Cr2L, Cr2R, K2] to end.
**3rd row** [P1, Cr2R, P2, Cr2L, P1] to end.
**4th row** [Cr2L, K4, Cr2R].
**5th row** K1, P6, [C2B, P6] to last st, K1.
**6th row** [Cr2R, K4, Cr2L] to end.
**7th row** [P1, Cr2L, P2, Cr2R, P1] to end.
**8th row** [K2, Cr2R, Cr2L, K2] to end.
These 8 rows form patt.

### HEART MOTIF
Worked over 13 sts.
**1st row** (right side) K3, P1, K5, P1, K3.
**2nd row** P2, K3, P3, K3, P2.
**3rd row** K1, [P2, K1] 4 times.
**4th row** K2, P3, K3, P3, K2.
**5th row** P2, K4, P1, K4, P2.
**6th row** P1, K2, P7, K2, P1.
**7th row** K2, P2, K5, P2, K2.
**8th row** P3, [K2, P3] twice.
**9th row** K4, P2, K1, P2, K4.
**10th row** P5, K3, P5.
**11th row** K6, P1, K6.
**12th row** P13.
**13th row** K13.
**14th row** P13.

15th and 16th rows As 13th and 14th rows.
17th row As 11th row.
18th row As 10th row.
19th row As 9th row.
20th row As 8th row.
21st row As 7th row.
22nd row As 6th row.
23rd row As 5th row.
24th row As 4th row.
25th row As 3rd row.
26th row As 2nd row.
27th row As 1st row.

## BACK

With 3 mm (No 11/US 2) needles, cast on 146(162) sts.
**Beg with a K row, work 7 rows in st st.
Next row (fold line) K.
Beg with a K row, work in st st until Back measures 32(37) cm/12½(14½) in from fold line, ending with a K row. **
Dec row P19(21), [P2 tog, P1] 36(40) times, P19(21). 110(122) sts.
Work in patt as follows:
1st row (right side) K18(20), P1, work 1st row of patt A across next 72(80) sts, P1, K18(20).
2nd row P18(20), K1, work 2nd row of patt A across next 72(80) sts, K1, P18(20).
Work a further 8 rows as set.
11th row K3(4), work 1st row of Heart Motif, K2(3), P1, work 72(80) sts in patt A, P1, K2(3), work 1st row of Heart Motif, K3(4).
12th row P3(4), work 2nd row of Heart Motif, P2(3), K1, work 72(80) sts in patt A, K1, P2(3), work 2nd row of Heart Motif, P3(4).
Work a further 25 rows as set.
38th row P18(20), K1, work 72(80) sts in patt A, K1, P18(20).
39th row K18(20), P1, work 72(80) sts in patt A, P1, K18(20).
Cont as now set until work measures 49(55) cm/19¼(21½) in from fold line, ending with a right side row.
Shape Neck and Shoulders
Next row Patt 44(49), cast off next 22(24) sts, patt to end.
Work on last set of sts only. Patt 1 row.
Cast off 5 sts at beg of next row, 16(18) sts at beg of foll row and 5 sts at beg of foll row. Cast off rem 18(21) sts.
With right side facing, rejoin yarn to rem sts and patt 2 rows. Cast off 5 sts at beg of next row, 16(18) sts at beg of foll row and 5 sts at beg of foll row. Cast off rem 18(21) sts.

## LEFT FRONT

With 3 mm (No 11/US 2) needles, cast on 69(77) sts.
Work as given for Back from ** to **.
Dec row [P2 tog] 1(2) times, [P1, P2 tog] 15 times, P1, [P2 tog] 1(3) times, P19(21). 52(57) sts.
Work in patt as follows:
1st row (right side) K18(20), P1, work 1st row of patt A across next 32 sts, P1(4).
2nd row K1(4), work 2nd row of patt A across next 32 sts, K1, P18(20).
Work a further 8 rows as set.

11th row K3(4), work 1st row of Heart Motif, K2(3), P1, work 32 sts in patt A, P1(4).
12th row K1(4), work 32 sts in patt A, K1, P2(3), work 2nd row of Heart Motif, P3(4).
Work a further 25 rows as set.
38th row K1(4), work 32 sts in patt A, K1, P18(20).
39th row K18(20), P1, work 32 sts in patt A, P1(4).
Cont as now set until work measures 45(51) cm/17¾(20) in from fold line, ending with a right side row.
Shape Neck
Keeping patt correct, cast off 9 sts at beg of next row. Dec one st at neck edge on every row until 34(39) sts rem. Cont straight until Front matches Back to shoulder shaping, ending with a wrong side row.
Shape Shoulder
Cast off 16(18) sts at beg of next row. Work 1 row. Cast off rem 18(21) sts.

## RIGHT FRONT

With 3 mm (No 11/US 2) needles, cast on 69(77) sts.
Work as given for Back from ** to **.
Dec row P19(21), [P2 tog] 1(3) times, P1, [P2 tog, P1] 15 times, [P2 tog] 1(2) times. 52(57) sts.
Work in patt as follows:
1st row (right side) P1(4), work 1st row of patt A across next 32 sts, P1, K18(20).
2nd row P18(20), K1, work 2nd row of patt A across next 32 sts, K1(4).
Work a further 8 rows as set.
11th row P1(4), work 32 sts in patt A, P1, K2(3), work 1st row of Heart Motif, K3(4).
12th row P3(4), work 2nd row of Heart Motif, P2(3), K1, work 32 sts in patt A, K1(4).
Work a further 25 rows as set.
38th row P18(20), K1, work 32 sts in patt A, K1(4).
39th row P1(4), work 32 sts in patt A, P1, K18(20).
Cont as now set and complete as given for Left Front, reversing shapings.

## SLEEVES

With 3 mm (No 11/US 2) needles, cast on 42(49) sts.
Beg with a K row, work 7 rows in st st.
Next row (fold line) K.
Inc row P4, *[K twice in next st, P6] 1(2) times, K twice in next st, P2, P twice in next st, P2; rep from * once, [K twice in next st, P6] 1(0) time, K twice in next st, P4. 50(58) sts.
Next row K1, work 2nd row of patt A across next 48(56) sts, K1.
Next row P1, work 3rd row of patt A across next 48(56) sts, P1.
Work a further 14 rows as set.
Inc row P1(2), [P twice in each of next 2 sts, P1] to last 1(2) sts, P1(2). 82(94) sts.
Beg with a K row, work in st st, inc one st at each end of 5th row and every foll 6th(8th) row until there are 92(104) sts.
Cont straight for a few rows until Sleeve measures 15(18) cm/6(7) in from fold line, ending with a P row.
Next row K21(23), P1, work 1st row of patt A across next 48(56) sts, P1,
K21(23).
Next row P21(23), K1, work 2nd row of patt A across next 48(56) sts, K1, P21(23).
Work a further 23 rows as set. Cast off.

## COLLAR

With 3 mm (No 11/US 2) needles, cast on 64(72) sts.
Beg with a K row, work 7 rows in st st inc one st at each end of 2nd row and every foll row. 76(84) sts.
Next row (fold line) K.
Next row P4, K twice in next st, P4, K58 (66), P4, K twice in next st, P4. 78(86) sts.
Work in patt as follows:
1st row (wrong side) K3, Cr2L, Cr2R, K3, P58(66), K3, Cr2L, P2, Cr2R, K3.
2nd row P2, Cr2R, P2, Cr2L, P2, K58(66), P2, Cr2R, P2, Cr2L, P2.
3rd row K1, Cr2L, K4, Cr2R, K1, P58(66), K1, Cr2L, K4, Cr2R, K1.
4th row P1, K1, P6, K1, P1, K58(66), P1, K1, P6, K1, P1.
5th row K1, Cr2R, K4, Cr2L, K1, P58(66), K1, Cr2R, K4, Cr2L, K1.
6th row P2, Cr2L, P2, Cr2R, P2, K58(66), P2, Cr2L, P2, Cr2R, P2.
7th row K3, Cr2R, Cr2L, K3, P58(66), K3, Cr2R, Cr2L, K3.
8th row P4, C2F, P4, K58(66), P4, C2F, P4.
These 8 rows form patt. Work a further 34(42) rows.
Shape Neck
Next row Patt 30(33), cast off next 18(20) sts, patt to end.
Cont on last set of sts only for right side of collar. Patt 1 row. Cast off 3 sts at beg of next row and foll alt row. 24(27) sts. Patt 11 rows straight. Inc one st at beg of next row and at same edge on every row until there are 31(34) sts. Patt 1 row. Cast on 8(9) sts at beg of next row. 39(43) sts.
Patt 28(36) rows straight.
Next row P4, K2 tog, P4, K29(33).
Next row (fold line) K.
Beg with a K row, work 7 rows in st st, dec one st at end of 2nd row and at same edge of every foll row. 32(36) sts. Cast off.
With right side facing, rejoin yarn to rem sts and patt to end. Complete to match first side, reversing shapings.

## COLLAR FACINGS

With 3 mm (No 11/US 2) needles and right side facing, pick up and K 67 (79) sts evenly along one outside edge between fold lines.
Next row (fold line) K.
Beg with a K row, work 7 rows in st st, dec one st at each end of 2nd row and every foll row. 55(67) sts. Cast off.
Work other outside edge in same way.
With 3 mm (No 11/US 2) needles and right side facing, pick up and K 21(27) sts evenly along inside edge between fold line and cast on sts at neck.
Next row (fold line) K.
Beg with a K row, work 7 rows in st st, dec one st at end of 2nd row and at same edge of every foll row. 15(21) sts. Cast off.

**POCKETS** (make 2)
With 3 mm (No 11/US 2) needles, cast on 30(32) sts. Beg with a K row, work 7 rows in st st.
**Next row** (fold line)  K.
Beg with a K row, work 36(40) rows in st st. Cast off.

**BUTTONHOLE BAND**
With 2¼ mm (No 13/US 0) needles and right side facing, pick up and K 120 (140) sts along front edge of Right Front from fold line to beg of neck shaping. Beg with a P row, work 2 rows in st st.

**1st buttonhole row**  P2, [cast off 2, P9(11) sts more] 6 times, P to end.
**2nd buttonhole row**  K to end, casting on 2 sts over those cast off in previous row. Work 3 rows in st st.
**Next row** (fold line)  P.
Beg with a P row, work 3 rows in st st.
**1st buttonhole row**  K56(66), [cast off 2, K9(11) sts more] 5 times, cast off 2, K1 st more.
**2nd buttonhole row**  P to end, casting on 2 sts over those cast off in previous row. Work 2 rows in st st. Cast off.

**BUTTON BAND**
Work to match Buttonhole Band, omitting buttonholes.

**TO MAKE UP**
Join shoulder seams. Sew on sleeves, placing centre of sleeves to shoulder seams. Join side and sleeve seams. Fold all hems and facings at fold line to wrong side and slip stitch in positions, joining open ends of front bands together and mitring corners of collar facings. Neaten buttonholes. Sew on pockets, collar and buttons.

# *Cable Sweater with Chicken Panel*

See Page
**18**

## MEASUREMENTS

| To fit age | 18–24 | 24–36 | Months |
|---|---|---|---|
| Actual chest measurement | 69 | 73 | cm |
|  | 27¼ | 28¾ | in |
| Length | 36 | 40 | cm |
|  | 14¼ | 15¾ | in |
| Sleeve seam | 20 | 23 | cm |
|  | 8 | 9 | in |

## MATERIALS
7(8) 50 g balls of Rowan DK Handknit Cotton in Orange (MC).
1(1) 50 g ball of same in each of Cream (A), Yellow (B) and Black (C).
Pair each of 3¼ mm (No 10/US 3) and 4 mm (No 8/US 5) knitting needles.
Cable needle.

## TENSION
20 sts and 28 rows to 10 cm/4 in square over st st on 4 mm (No 8/US 5) needles.

## ABBREVIATIONS
Cr4L = slip next 3 sts onto cable needle and leave at front of work, K1, then K1 tbl, P1, K1 tbl sts from cable needle;
Cr4R = slip next st onto cable needle

and leave at back of work, K1 tbl, P1, K1 tbl, then K1 from cable needle;
C7F = slip next 3 sts onto cable needle and leave at front of work, [K1 tbl, P1] twice, then K1 tbl, P1, K1 tbl sts from cable needle;
MB = make bobble, [K1, yf, K1, yf, K1] all in next st, turn, P5, turn, K3, K2 tog, then pass 2nd, 3rd and 4th st over first st.
Also see page 5.

## NOTE
Read Charts from right to left on right side rows and from left to right on wrong side rows. When working motifs, use separate lengths of A, B and C yarn for each coloured area and twist yarns together on wrong side when changing colour to avoid holes.

## PANEL A – Worked over 21 sts.
**1st row** (wrong side)  K7, P1, K1, P3, K1, P1, K7.
**2nd row**  P6, Cr4R, K1 tbl, Cr4L, P6.
**3rd row**  K6, [P1, K1] 4 times, P1, K6.
**4th row**  P5, Cr4R, K1, K1 tbl, K1, Cr4L, P5.
**5th row**  K5, P1, K1, [P1, K2] twice, P1, K1, P1, K5.
**6th row**  P4, Cr4R, K2, K1 tbl, K2, Cr4L, P4.

**7th row**  K4, P1, K1, P2, K2, P1, K2, P2, K1, P1, K4.
**8th row**  P3, Cr4R, [K1 tbl, K2] twice, K1 tbl, Cr4L, P3.
**9th row**  K3, [P1, K1] twice, [P1, K2] twice, [P1, K1] twice, P1, K3.
**10th row**  P2, Cr4R, K1, [K1 tbl, K2] twice, K1 tbl, K1, Cr4L, P2.
**11th row**  K2, P1, K1, [P1, K2] 4 times, P1, K1, P1, K2.
**12th row**  P1, Cr4R, [K2, K1 tbl] 3 times,

K2, Cr4L, P1.
**13th row**  [K1, P1] twice, K3, [P1, K2] 3 times, K1, [P1, K1] twice.
**14th row**  [P1, K1 tbl] twice, K3, [MB, K2] 3 times, K1, [K1 tbl, P1] twice.
**15th row**  [K1, P1] twice, K3, [P1 tbl, K2] 3 times, K1, [P1, K1] twice.
**16th row**  [P1, K1 tbl] twice, P3, K1 tbl, P1, K3 tbl, P1, K1 tbl, P3,[K1 tbl, P1] twice.
These 16 rows form patt.

## PANEL B – Worked over 13 sts.
**1st row** (wrong side)  P1 tbl, K2, [P1 tbl, K1] 4 times, K1, P1 tbl.
**2nd row**  K1 tbl, P2, C7F, P2, K1 tbl.
**3rd row**  As 1st row.
**4th row**  K1 tbl, P2, [K1 tbl, P1] 4 times, P1, K1 tbl.
**5th to 10th rows**  Rep 3rd and 4th rows 3 times.
These 10 rows form patt.

## BACK
With 3¼ mm (No 10/US 3) needles and MC, cast on 65(69) sts.
**1st row** (wrong side)  K1, [P1 tbl, K1] to end.
**2nd row**  P1, [K1 tbl, P1] to end.
Rep last 2 rows until work measures 4 cm/1½ in from beg, ending with a wrong side row and inc 4 sts evenly across last row. 69(73) sts.
Change to 4 mm (No 8/US 5) needles.
Work border patt as follows:
**1st row**  K in MC.
**2nd row**  P in MC. **
**3rd row**  K7(9)MC, [K across 1st row of Chart 1, K8MC] twice, K across 1st row of Chart 1, K7(9)MC.
**4th row**  P7(9)MC, [P across 2nd row of Chart 1, P8MC] twice, P across 2nd row of Chart 1, P7(9)MC.
**5th to 17th rows**  Rep 3rd and 4th rows 6 times, then work 3rd row again but working 3rd to 15th rows of Chart 1.
*** **18th row**  P in MC.

19th and 20th rows As 1st and 2nd rows.

Cont in MC only.

Inc row K0(2), [K twice in next st, K1, K twice in next st, K2] 13 times, [K twice in next st, K1(2)] twice. 97(101) sts.

Work in main patt as follows:

1st row (wrong side) K1, [P1, K1] 1(2) times, P1 tbl, [work 1st row of Panel A, then Panel B] twice, work 1st row of Panel A, P1 tbl, [K1, P1] 1(2) times, K1.

2nd row P1, [K1, P1] 1(2) times, K1 tbl, [work 2nd row of Panel A, then Panel B] twice, work 2nd row of Panel A, K1 tbl, [P1, K1] 1(2) times, P1.

3rd row P1, [K1, P1] 1(2) times, P1 tbl, [work 3rd row of Panel A, then Panel B] twice, work 3rd row of Panel A, P1 tbl, [P1, K1] 1(2) times, P1.

4th row K1, [P1, K1] 1(2) times, K1 tbl, [work 4th row of Panel A, then Panel B] twice, work 4th row of Panel A, K1 tbl, [K1, P1] 1(2) times, K1.

These 4 rows set position of Panels and form double moss st at each side. ***

Cont in patt as set until work measures 36(40) cm/14¼(15¾) in from beg, ending with a wrong side row.

Shape Shoulders

Cast off 14(15) sts at beg of next 2 rows and 14 sts at beg of foll 2 rows.

Leave rem 41(43) sts on a holder.

### FRONT

Work as given for Back to **.

3rd row K6(8)MC, K across 1st row of Chart 2, K7MC, K across 1st row of Chart 1, K8MC, K across 1st row of Chart 1, K7(9)MC.

4th row P7(9)MC, P across 2nd row of Chart 1, P8MC, P across 2nd row of Chart 1, P7MC, P across 2nd row of Chart 2, P6(8)MC.

5th to 10th rows Rep 3rd and 4th rows 3 times, but working 3rd to 8th rows of Charts.

11th row K28(30)MC, K across 9th row of Chart 1, K8MC, K across 9th row of Chart 1, K7(9)MC.

12th row P7(9)MC, P across 10th row of Chart 1, P8MC, P across 10th row of Chart 1, P28(30)MC.

13th to 17th rows Rep 11th and 12th rows twice, then work 11th row again, but working 11th to 15th rows of Chart 1.

Work as given for Back from *** to ***.

Cont in patt as set until work measures 30(34) cm/11¾(13¼) in from beg, ending with a wrong side row.

Shape Neck

Next row Patt 39(40), turn.

Work on this set of sts only. Keeping patt correct, dec one st at neck edge on every row until 28(29) sts rem. Cont straight until Front matches Back to shoulders, ending at side edge.

Shape Shoulder

Cast off 14(15) sts at beg of next row. Patt 1 row. Cast off rem 15 sts.

With right side facing, slip centre 19(21) sts onto a holder, rejoin yarn to rem sts and patt to end. Complete to match first side.

### SLEEVES

With 3¼ mm (No 10/US 3) needles and MC, cast on 43(47) sts. Work 5 cm/2 in in rib as given for Back welt, ending with a wrong side row.

Inc row Rib 4(6), inc in next st, rib 7, inc in next st, [rib 2, inc in next st] twice, rib 2, work 3 times in next st, rib 2, [inc in next st, rib 2] twice, inc in next st, rib 7, inc in next st, rib 4(6). 53(57) sts.

Change to 4 mm (No 8/US 5) needles.

Work in patt as follows:

1st row P1, [K1, P1] 1(2) times, work 1st row of Panel B, Panel A, then Panel B, [P1, K1] 1(2) times, P1.

2nd row K1, [P1, K1] 1(2) times, work 2nd row of Panel B, Panel A, then Panel B, [K1, P1] 1(2) times, K1.

3rd row K1, [P1, K1] 1(2) times, work 3rd row of Panel B, Panel A, then Panel B, [K1, P1] 1(2) times, K1.

4th row P1, [K1, P1] 1(2) times, work 4th row of Panel B, Panel A, then Panel B, [P1, K1] 1(2) times, P1.

These 4 rows set position of Panels and form double moss st at each side.

Cont in patt as set, inc one st at each end of next row and every foll alt row until there are 81(85) sts, working inc sts into double moss st.

Cont straight until Sleeve measures 20(23) cm/8(9) in from beg, ending with a wrong side row. Cast off.

### NECKBAND

Join right shoulder seam.

With 3¼ mm (No 10/US 3) needles, MC and right side facing, pick up and K 16 sts down left front neck, K across centre front sts, pick up and K 15 sts up right front neck, K back neck sts. 91(95) sts.

Beg with a 1st row, work 11 rows in rib as given for Back welt. Cast off in rib.

### TO MAKE UP

Join left shoulder and neckband seam. Sew on sleeves, placing centre of sleeves to shoulder seams. Join side and sleeve seams. With B, embroider beaks on hens and chicks. With C, embroider chicks' eyes.

CHART 1

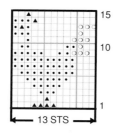

13 STS

CHART 2

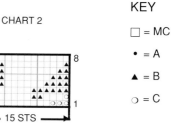

15 STS

KEY

☐ = MC

• = A

▲ = B

○ = C

# Cow Sweater

See Page
*19*

## MEASUREMENTS

| To fit age | 6–12 | 12–18 | Months |
|---|---|---|---|
| Actual chest measurement | 69 | 75 | cm |
| | 27 | 29½ | in |
| Length | 29 | 32 | cm |
| | 11½ | 12½ | in |
| Sleeve seam | 19 | 22 | cm |
| | 7½ | 8½ | in |

## MATERIALS

4(5) 50 g balls of Rowan Cotton Glace in Black (MC).
2(3) 50 g balls of same in Cream (A).
1(1) 50 g ball of same in Green.
Small amount of 4 ply cotton in Pink.
Pair each of 2¾ mm (No 12/US 1) and 3¼ mm (No 10/US 3) knitting needles.
6 buttons.

## TENSION

26 sts and 30 rows to 10 cm/4 in square over check pattern on 3¼ mm (No 10/US 3) needles.

## ABBREVIATIONS

See page 5.

## NOTE

Read Chart from right to left on right side rows and from left to right on wrong side rows. When working check pattern, strand yarn not in use loosely across wrong side to keep fabric elastic. When working motif, use separate small balls of yarn for each coloured area and twist yarns together on wrong side when changing colour to avoid holes.

## FRONT

With 2¾ mm (No 12/US 1) needles and MC, cast on 83(91) sts.
**1st row** (right side) K1, [P1, K1] to end.
**2nd row** P1, [K1, P1] to end.
Rep last 2 rows until welt measures 3 cm/1¼ in from beg, ending with a right side row.
**Inc row** Rib 8(6), inc in next st, [rib 10(12), inc in next st] 6 times, rib 8(6). 90(98) sts.
Change to 3¼ mm (No 10/US 3) needles.
Work in check patt as follows:
**1st row** (right side) K3A, [4MC, 4A] to last 7 sts, 4MC, 3A.
**2nd row** P3A, [4MC, 4A] to last 7 sts, 4MC, 3A.
**3rd and 4th rows** As 1st and 2nd rows.
**5th row** K3MC, [4A, 4MC] to last 7 sts, 4A, 3MC.
**6th row** P3MC, [4A, 4MC] to last 7 sts, 4A, 3MC.
**7th and 8th rows** As 5th and 6th rows.
These 8 rows form check patt.** Cont in check patt, work a further 16(20) rows.
Place motif as follows:
**Next row** Patt 27(31), K across 1st row of Chart, patt 27(31).
**Next row** Patt 27(31), P across 2nd row of Chart, patt 27(31).
Cont working from Chart as set until 32nd row of Chart has been worked.
Work in check patt across all sts until Front measures 24(27) cm/9½(10½) in from beg, ending with a wrong side row.
**Shape Neck**
**Next row** Patt 36(39), turn.
Work on this set of sts only. Keeping patt correct, dec one st at neck edge on every row until 31(34) sts rem. Cont straight until

Front measures 28(31) cm/11(12) in from beg, ending with a wrong side row. Leave these sts on a spare needle.
With right side facing, slip centre 18(20) sts onto a holder, rejoin yarn to rem sts, patt to end. Complete to match first side.

## BACK

Work as given for Front to **.
Cont in check patt until Back measures 26(29) cm/10¼(11¼) in from beg, ending with a wrong side row.
**Shape Neck**
**Next row** Patt 36(39), turn.
Work on this set of sts only. Dec one st at neck edge on next 5 rows. 31(34) sts.
Leave these sts on a spare needle.
With right side facing, slip centre 18(20)

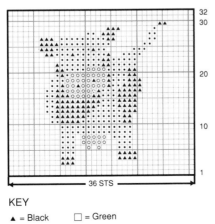

32
30

20

10

1

— 36 STS —

**KEY**

▲ = Black    □ = Green
• = Cream    ○ = Pink

sts onto a holder, rejoin yarn to rem sts, patt to end. Complete to match first side.

## SLEEVES

With 2¾ mm (No 12/US 1) needles and MC, cast on 37(41) sts. Work 3 cm/1¼ in in rib as given for Front welt, ending with a right side row.
**Inc row** Rib 7(5), [inc in next st, rib 5(3)] to end. 42(50) sts.
Change to 3¼ mm (No 10/US 3) needles. Work in check patt as given for Front, inc one st at each end of 5(10) foll 2nd(3rd) rows, then on every foll 3rd(4th) row until there are 70(78) sts, working inc sts into patt.
Cont straight until Sleeve measures 19(22) cm/7½(8½) in from beg, ending with a wrong side row. Cast off.

## BACK NECKBAND

With 2¾ mm (No 12/US 1) needles, MC and right side facing, pick up and K 6 sts down right back neck, K across back neck sts dec one st, pick up and K 6 sts up left back neck. 29(31) sts. Beg with a 2nd row, work 7 rows in rib as given for Front welt. Cast off in rib.

## FRONT NECKBAND

With 2¾ mm (No 12/US 1) needles, MC and right side facing, pick up and K 14 sts down left front neck, K across front neck sts dec one st, pick up and K 14 sts up right front neck. 45(47) sts. Complete as given for Back Neckband.

## BUTTONHOLE BANDS

With 2¾ mm (No 12/US 1) needles, MC and right side facing, K across left front shoulder sts, dec 2(3) sts evenly then pick up and K 6 sts along row ends of neckband. 35(37) sts. Beg with a 2nd row, work 3 rows in rib as given for Front welt.
**1st buttonhole row** Rib 5, [cast off 2, rib until there are 10(11) sts] twice, cast off 2, rib until there are 4 sts.
**2nd buttonhole row** Rib to end, casting on 2 sts over those cast off in previous row.
Rib 3 rows. Cast off in rib.
Work right front shoulder to match.

## BUTTON BANDS

With 2¾ mm (No 12/US 1) needles, MC and right side facing, K across right back shoulder sts, dec 2(3) sts evenly then pick up and K 6 sts along row ends of neckband. 35(37) sts. Beg with a 2nd row, work 8 rows in rib as given for Front welt. Cast off in rib.
Work left back shoulder to match.

## TO MAKE UP

Lap buttonhole bands over button bands and catch down at side edges. Sew on sleeves, placing centre of sleeves in line with buttonholes. Join side and sleeve seams. Sew on buttons.

# Hen and Chick Cardigan

See Page
## 20

| MEASUREMENTS To fit age | 1 | 2 | Years |
|---|---|---|---|
| Actual chest measurement | 72 28¼ | 78 30½ | cm in |
| Length to shoulder | 31 12¼ | 34 13½ | cm in |
| Sleeve seam | 21 8¼ | 25 10 | cm in |

## MATERIALS
6(6) 50 g balls of Rowan DK Handknit Cotton in Blue (MC).
1(1) 50 g ball of same in each of Yellow (A), Red (B) and Cream (C).
Pair of 4 mm (No 8/US 5) knitting needles.
Medium size crochet hook.
3 buttons.

## TENSION
20 sts and 28 rows to 10 cm/4 in square over st st on 4 mm (No 8/US 5) needles.

## ABBREVIATIONS
Ch = chain; dc = double crochet; tr = treble; ss = slip stitch.
Also see page 5 .

## NOTE
Read Charts from right to left on K rows and from left to right on P rows. Use separate lengths of A, B and C yarn for each motif and twist yarns together on wrong side when changing colour to avoid holes. If preferred the motifs may be Swiss Darned when knitting is complete.

CHART 1

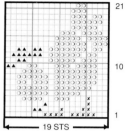

21
10
1
19 STS

CHART 2

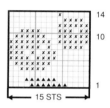

14
10
1
15 STS

KEY
□ = MC    x = A    ▲ = B    ○ = C

## BACK
With 4 mm (No 8/US 5) needles and MC, cast on 72(78) sts.
Beg with a K row, work in st st until Back measures 17(19) cm/6¾ (7½) in from beg, ending with a P row.
### Shape Armholes
Cast off 4(5) sts at beg of next 2 rows. 64(68) sts. Cont straight until Back measures 30(33) cm/12(13¼) in from beg, ending with a P row.
### Shape Shoulders
Cast off 10(11) sts at beg of next 2 rows and 10 sts at beg of foll 2 rows. Cast off rem 24(26) sts.

## LEFT FRONT
With 4 mm (No 8/US 5) needles and MC, cast on 34(37) sts.
Beg with a K row, work 14 rows in st st.**
Place Hen motif as follows:
**1st row** (right side) K11(14)MC, K across 1st row of Chart 1, K4MC.
**2nd row** P4MC, P across 2nd row of Chart 1, P11(14)MC.
Work a further 19 rows from Chart 1 as set.
Now cont in st st and MC only until Front measures 15(17) cm/6(6¾) in from beg, ending with a P row.
### Shape Front
Dec one st at end (front edge) of next row and foll 3rd row. Work 2 rows.
### Shape Armhole
**Next row** Cast off 4(5) sts, K to last 2 sts, K2 tog. 27(29) sts.
Keeping armhole edge straight, cont to dec at front edge on every foll 3rd row until 20(21) sts rem.
Cont straight until Front matches Back to shoulder shaping, ending with a P row.
### Shape Shoulder
Cast off 10(11) sts at beg of next row. Work 1 row. Cast off rem 10 sts.

## RIGHT FRONT
Work as for Left Front to **.
Place Chick motif as follows:
**1st row** (right side) K6MC, K across 1st row of Chart 2, K13(16)MC.
**2nd row** P13(16)MC, P across 2nd row of Chart 2, P6MC.
Work a further 12 rows from Chart 2 as set. Complete to match Left Front, reversing shapings.

## SLEEVES
With 4 mm (No 8/US 5) needles and MC, cast on 40(44) sts.
Beg with a K row, work in st st, inc one st at each end of 3rd row and every foll 6th(7th) row until there are 54(58) sts.
Cont straight until Sleeve measures 22(27) cm/8¾(10¾) in from beg, ending with a P row. Cast off.

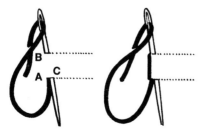

**Satin Stitch.** Bring needle out of A. Insert at B and emerge at C ready for next stitch.

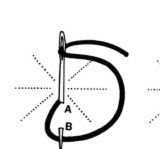

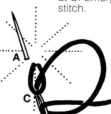

**Lazy Daisy Stitch.** Bring needle out at A. Insert back at A and emerge at B, looping yarn under the tip of needle. Pull needle through and over loop and insert at C. Emerge at A for next chain stitch.

## TO MAKE UP

Work Swiss Darning (see diagram page 70) if necessary. Join shoulder seams. Sew on sleeves, placing centre of sleeves to shoulder seams and sewing ends of last 6(8) rows to cast off sts at armholes. Join side and sleeve seams.

### Crochet Edging

With right side facing and crochet hook, join MC yarn to Right Front side seam.

Work 1 round of dc (the number of dc should be divisible by 3) along cast on edge of Right Front, front edge to shoulder, across back neck, down front edge of Left Front, then along cast on edge of Left Front and Back, working 3 dc in each corner, ss in first dc.

**Next round** [2 tr in same dc as ss, miss 2 dc, ss in next dc] to end, making 3 buttonhole loops along straight edge of Right Front by working 3 ch, miss 2 dc, ss in next dc. Fasten off.

Work crochet edging along lower edge of sleeves. With A, B or C, embroider flowers in lazy daisy stitch (see diagrams) along lower edge of Back, Fronts and Sleeves. Fill centre of flowers with B or A and satin st (see diagrams). With B, embroider beaks. Sew on buttons.

# Farmyard Picture Book Sweater

See Page

*21*

## MEASUREMENTS

| To fit age | 18–24 | 24–36 | Months |
|---|---|---|---|
| Actual chest measurement | 70 | 78 | cm |
| | 27½ | 30¾ | in |
| Length | 38 | 40 | cm |
| | 15 | 15¾ | in |
| Sleeve seam | 20 | 24 | cm |
| | 8 | 9½ | in |

## MATERIALS

5(6) 50 g balls of Rowan DK Handknit Cotton in Red (MC).
1(1) 50 g ball of same in each of Cream, Yellow, Black, Dark Pink, Blue, Green and Light Pink.
Pair each of 3¼ mm (No 10/US 3) and 4 mm (No 8/US 5) knitting needles.

## TENSION

20 sts and 28 rows to 10 cm/4 in square over st st on 4 mm (No 8/US 5) needles.

## ABBREVIATIONS

See page 5.

## NOTE

Read Chart from right to left on right side rows and from left to right on wrong side rows. When working in pattern, use separate small balls of yarn for each coloured area and twist yarns together on wrong side when changing colour to avoid holes.

## BACK

With 3¼ mm (No 10/US 3) needles and MC, cast on 66(74) sts.
**1st row** (right side) K2, [P2, K2] to end.
**2nd row** P2, [K2, P2] to end.
Rep last 2 rows until work measures 4 cm/1½ in from beg, ending with a wrong side row and inc 4 sts evenly across last row. 70(78) sts.
Change to 4 mm (No 8/US 5) needles.
Beg with a K row, work 2(4) rows in st st.
Cont in st st and patt from Chart until 92nd row of Chart has been worked.
Cont in MC only, work 2(6) rows.
### Shape Shoulders
Cast off 10(11) sts at beg of next 2 rows and 10(12) sts at beg of foll 2 rows. Leave rem 30(32) sts on a holder.

## FRONT

Work as given for Back until 84th row of Chart has been worked.
### Shape Neck

**Next row** Patt 26(29), K2 tog, turn.
Work on this set of sts only. Keeping patt correct, dec one st at neck edge on every row until 20(23) sts rem, ending with 92nd row of Chart.
Cont in MC only, work 2(6) rows straight.
### Shape Shoulder
Cast off 10(11) sts at beg of next row.
Work 1 row. Cast off rem 10(12) sts.
With right side facing, slip centre 14(16) sts onto a holder, rejoin MC yarn to rem sts, K2 tog, K to end. Complete to match first side, reversing shoulder shaping.

## LEFT SLEEVE

With 3¼ mm (No 10/US 3) needles and MC, cast on 34(38) sts. Work 5 cm/2 in in rib as given for Back welt, ending with a right side row.
**Inc row** Rib 2(5), inc in next st, [rib 3, inc in next st] to last 3(4) sts, rib 3(4). 42(46) sts.
Change to 4 mm (No 8/US 5) needles.

Beg with a K row, work 10(14) rows in st st inc one st at each end of 3rd row and 3(5) foll alt rows. 50(58) sts. **
Place sheep motif as follows:
**Next row** With MC, K twice in first st, K10(14), K 6th(10th) to 32nd(36th) sts of 12th row of Chart for Back, with MC, K to last st, K twice in last st.
**Next row** P13(17) MC, P 39th(43rd) to 65th(69th) sts of 13th row of Chart for Back, with MC, P to end.
These 2 rows set the patt. Cont as set until 33rd row of Chart has been worked, at the same time, inc one st at each end of next row and every foll 2nd(3rd) row until there are 70(74) sts, working inc sts in MC. With MC only, work 10(18) rows.
Cast off.

## RIGHT SLEEVE

Work as given for Left Sleeve to **.
Place cow motif as follows:
**Next row** With MC, K twice in first st, K9(13), K 34th(38th) to 63rd(67th) sts of 58th row of Chart for Back, with MC, K to last st, K twice in last st.
**Next row** P11(15)MC, P 8th(12th) to 37th(41st) sts of 59th row of Chart for Back, with MC, P to end.
These 2 rows set the patt. Cont as set until 81st row of Chart has been worked, at the same time, inc one st at each end of next row and every foll 2nd(3rd) row until there are 70(74) sts, working inc sts in MC. With MC, work 8(16) rows.
Cast off.

## NECKBAND

Join right shoulder seam.
With 3¼ mm (No 10/US 3) needles, MC and right side facing, pick up and K16(18) sts down left front neck, K centre front neck sts, pick up and K16(18) sts up right front neck, K back neck sts. 76(84) sts. Work 12 rows in K2, P2 rib. Cast off in rib.

## TO MAKE UP

Join left shoulder and neckband seam. Sew on sleeves, placing centre of sleeves to shoulder seams. Join side and sleeve seams. With Black, embroider feet and

## KEY

☐ = Red

○ = Cream

– = Yellow

▲ = Black

❘ = Dark Pink

• = Blue

v = Green

✳ = Light Pink

∧, ⋋ or ╱ =

embroidery
sts

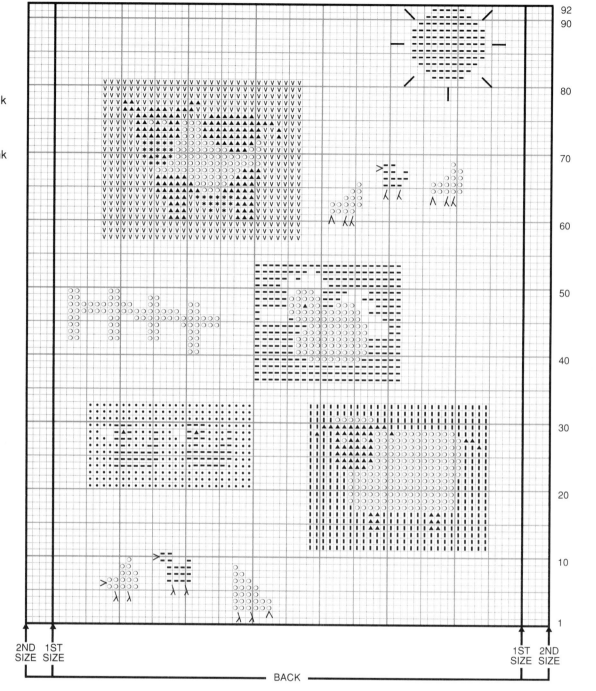

2ND
SIZE   1ST
SIZE

1ST
SIZE   2ND
SIZE

92
90
80
70
60
50
40
30
20
10
1

—————— BACK ——————

eyes on chicks. Embroider chicks' beaks
in Black or Yellow. With Yellow, work a
few straight stitches (see diagram)
around the sun for rays.

**Straight Stitch.** Bring needle out to front
at A, insert at B. This stitch can be any
length and work in any direction.

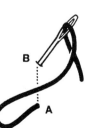

See Front Cover

# Hen Sweater

## MEASUREMENTS

| To fit age | 2–4 | 4–6 | Years |
|---|---|---|---|
| Actual chest measurement | 80 | 88 | cm |
| | 31½ | 34½ | in |
| Length | 46 | 51 | cm |
| | 18 | 20 | in |
| Sleeve seam | 25 | 30 | cm |
| | 10 | 12 | in |

## MATERIALS
8(9) 50 g balls of Rowan DK Handknit Cotton in Blue (MC).
1(1) 50 g ball of same in each of Black, Red, Green, White, Rust, Pink and Yellow.
Pair each of 3¼ mm (No 10/US 3) and 4 mm (No 8/US 5) knitting needles.

## TENSION
20 sts and 28 rows to 10 cm/4 in square over st st on 4 mm (No 8/US 5) needles.

## ABBREVIATIONS
See page 5.

## NOTE
Read Charts from right to left on right side rows and from left to right on wrong side rows. When working motif, use separate small balls or lengths of contrast yarn for each coloured area and twist yarns together on wrong side when changing colour to avoid holes.

## FRONT
** With 3¼ mm (No 10/US 3) needles and MC, cast on 74(82) sts.
**1st row** (right side) K2, [P2, K2] to end.
**2nd row** P2, [K2, P2] to end.
Rep last 2 rows 4(6) times more.
Change to 4 mm (No 8/US 5) needles.
**Next row** Cast on 3 sts for top of slit, K to end.
**Next row** Cast on 3 sts for top of slit, P to end. 80(88) sts.
Cont in st st and patt from Chart 1 until 32nd row of Chart 1 has been worked. **
With MC, work 4(8) rows in st st.
Place motif as follows:

**Next row** K10(14)MC, K across 1st row of Chart 2, K14(18)MC.
**Next row** P14(18)MC, P across 2nd row of Chart 2, P10(14)MC.
Cont working from Chart 2 as set until 59th row of Chart 2 has been worked.
Cont in st st and MC only for a few rows until Front measures 40(45) cm/15¾(17¾) in from beg, ending with a P row.
### Shape Neck
**Next row** Patt 32(35), turn.
Work on this set of sts only. Dec one st at neck edge on every row until 24(26) sts rem. Cont straight until Front measures 46(51) cm/18(20) in from beg, ending at

side edge.
### Shape Shoulder
Cast off 12(13) sts at beg of next row. Work 1 row. Cast off rem 12(13) sts.
With right side facing, slip centre 16(18) sts onto a holder, rejoin yarn to rem sts and K to end. Complete to match first side.

## BACK
Work as given for Front from ** to **. With MC, cont in st st until Back measures same as Front to shoulder shaping, ending with a P row.
### Shape Shoulders
Cast off 12(13) sts at beg of next 4 rows. Leave rem 32(36) sts on a holder.

## SLEEVES
With 3¼ mm (No 10/US 3) needles and MC, cast on 34(38) sts. Work 5 cm/2 in in rib as given for Front welt, ending with a right side row.
**Inc row** Rib 2(6), [m1, rib 4] 8 times. 42(46) sts.
Change to 4 mm (No 8/US 5) needles.
Beg with a K row, work 2 rows in st st.
Work in patt from Chart 1 as follows:
**Next row** Work from 20th(22nd) st to 61st(67th) st of 15th row of Chart 1.
**Next row** Work from 20th(22nd) st to 61st(67th) st of 16th row of Chart 1.
Work a further 17 rows as set, **at the same time**, inc one st at each end of next row and 5(4) foll 3rd(4th) rows, working inc sts in MC on first 15 rows and in patt on last 2 rows. 54(56) sts.
Cont in st st and MC only, inc one st at each end of 2nd(4th) row and every foll 3rd(4th) row until there are 70(74) sts.
Cont straight until Sleeve measures 25(30) cm/10(12) in from beg, ending with a P row. Cast off.

CHART 1

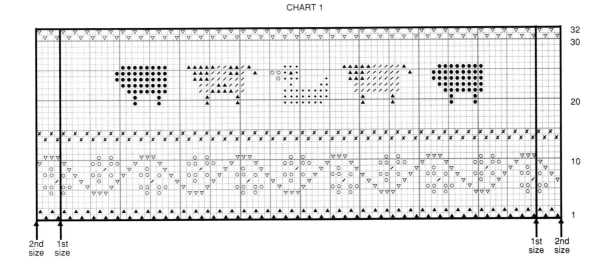

| | 32 |
| | 30 |
| | 20 |
| | 10 |
| | 1 |

2nd size    1st size                              1st size    2nd size

## NECKBAND

Join right shoulder seam.
With 3¼ mm (No 10/US 3) needles, MC and right side facing, pick up and K 19 sts down left front neck, K across centre front sts, pick up and K 19 sts up right front neck, K across back neck sts, dec 2 sts evenly across on **2nd** size only. 86(90) sts.
Beg with a 2nd row, work 18 rows in rib as given for Front welt. Cast off in rib.

## SLIT EDGINGS

With 3¼ mm (No 10/US 3) needles, MC and right side facing, pick up and K 8(12) sts from lower edge to top of slit at right side edge of Back.
Work 4 rows in K2, P2 rib. Cast off in rib.
Work left side of Back to match, reversing rib.
Work Front edges in same way.

## TO MAKE UP

Join left shoulder and neckband seam. Sew on sleeves, placing centre of sleeves to shoulder seams. Join row ends of slit edgings to top of slits. Beg at top of slits, join side seams, then sleeve seams. Embroider pig's eyes with Black and tail with Pink.

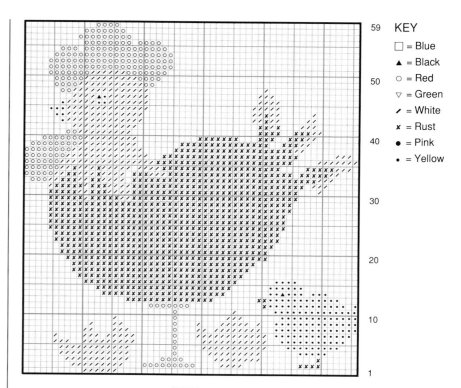

CHART 2

KEY

□ = Blue
▲ = Black
○ = Red
▽ = Green
✔ = White
x = Rust
● = Pink
• = Yellow

# *Mexican Sweater*

See Page
22

| MEASUREMENTS To fit age | 2–3 | Years |
|---|---|---|
| Actual chest measurement | 78 | **cm** |
| | 30¾ | **in** |
| Length | 37 | **cm** |
| | 14½ | **in** |
| Sleeve seam | 22 | **cm** |
| | 8¾ | **in** |

## MATERIALS

6 × 50 g balls of Rowan DK Handknit Cotton in Blue (MC).
1 × 50 g ball of same in each of Red (A), Brown, Green, Pink, Yellow, White and Black.
Pair each of 3¾ mm (No 9/US 4) and 4 mm (No 8/US 5) knitting needles.
4 Mexican dolls.

## TENSION

20 sts and 28 rows to 10 cm/4 in square over st st on 4 mm (No 8/US 5) needles.

## ABBREVIATIONS

See page 5.

## NOTE

Read Charts from right to left on right side rows and from left to right on wrong side rows. When working in pattern, use separate lengths of contrast yarns for each coloured area and twist yarns together on wrong side when changing colour to avoid holes.

## BACK

With 3¾ mm (No 9/US 4) needles and MC, cast on 78 sts.
Stranding yarn not·in use loosely across

wrong side of work, work in rib patt as follows:
**1st row** (right side) P2MC, [K2A, P2MC] to end.

**2nd row** K2MC, [P2A, K2MC] to end.
Rep last 2 rows until welt measures 4 cm/1½ in from beg, ending with a wrong side row.
Change to 4 mm (No 8/US 5) needles.
Beg with a K row, work in st st and patt from Chart 1 until 92nd row of Chart 1 has been worked.
**Shape Shoulders**
With MC, cast off 24 sts at beg of next 2 rows. Leave rem 30 sts on a holder.

## FRONT

Work as given for Back until 76th row of Chart 1 has been worked.
**Shape Neck**
**Next row** Patt 31, turn.
Work on this set of sts only. Cont working from Chart 1, cast off 2 sts at beg of next row and foll alt row. Dec one st at neck edge on 3 foll alt rows. 24 sts. Patt 6 rows straight. With MC, cast off.
With right side facing, slip centre 16 sts onto a holder, rejoin yarn to rem sts and patt to end. Patt 1 row. Complete to match first side.

## SLEEVES

With 3¾ mm (No 9/US 4) needles and MC, cast on 46 sts. Work 4 cm/1½ in in rib as given for Back welt, ending with a right side row.
**Inc row** Rib 4, [work twice in next st, rib 7] 5 times, work twice in next st, rib 1.

52 sts.
Change to 4 mm (No 8/US 5) needles.
Beg with a K row, work in st st and patt
from Chart 2, inc one st at each end of 5th
row and every foll 4th row until there are
72 sts. Cont straight until 50th row of
Chart 2 has been worked. Cast off.

## NECKBAND

Join right shoulder seam.
With 3¾ mm (No 9/US 4) needles, MC and
right side facing, pick up and K 16 sts
down left front neck, K centre front sts,
pick up and K 16 sts up right front neck,
K back neck sts. 78 sts. P 1 row.
Beg with a 1st row, work 6 rows in rib as
given for Back welt.
With MC, cast off in rib.

## TO MAKE UP

Join left shoulder and neckband seam.
Sew on sleeves, placing centre of sleeves
to shoulder seams. Join side and sleeve
seams. With Black, outline baskets,
melons, butterfly wings and heads, trees,
houses and house features. With Yellow,
work chain st (see diagram page 72)
between butterfly wings for body and 2
straight sts (see diagram page 56) with
French Knot (see diagram) at end of each
for antennae. Work few French Knots in
Red, Yellow or Green in baskets for fruit
and in Red on trees.
With Yellow, work straight sts around sun
for rays. Sew Mexican dolls in the area as
indicated by dotted lines on Chart 1.

**French Knot.** Bring needle out at A.
Wind yarn around it twice. Turn,
pulling twists tightly against needle.
Insert back into hole from which it
emerged. Pull yarn through to back.

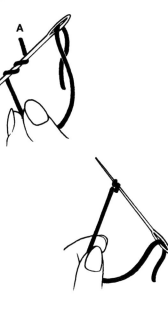

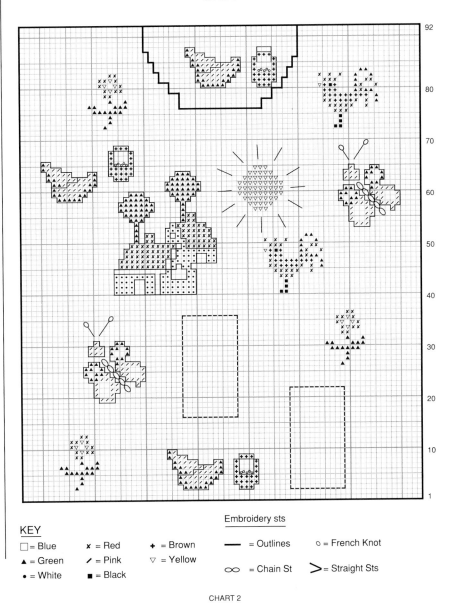

CHART 1

### KEY

□ = Blue    ✗ = Red    + = Brown

▲ = Green    ╱ = Pink    ▽ = Yellow

● = White    ■ = Black

**Embroidery sts**

— = Outlines    ○ = French Knot

∞ = Chain St    ⟩ = Straight Sts

CHART 2

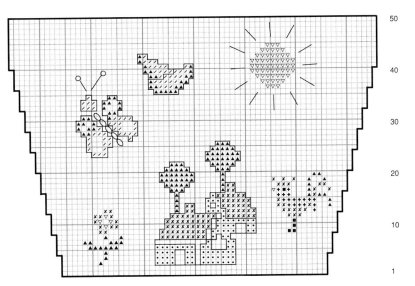

# Patchwork Sweater

See Page
*23*

## MEASUREMENTS

| To fit age | 2–3 | 3–4 | 4–5 | Years |
|---|---|---|---|---|
| Actual chest measurement | 72 | 78 | 84 | cm |
| | 28¼ | 30¾ | 33 | in |
| Length | 44 | 47 | 50 | cm |
| | 17¼ | 18½ | 19¾ | in |
| Sleeve seam | 27 | 29 | 31 | cm |
| | 10¾ | 11½ | 12¼ | in |

## MATERIALS
6(6:7) 50 g balls of Rowan DK Handknit Cotton in Cream (MC).
2(2:2) 50 g balls of same in Blue.
1(1:1) 50 g ball of same in each of Rust, Red, Brown and Pink.
Pair each of 3¼ mm (No 10/US 3) and 4 mm (No 8/US 5) knitting needles.

## TENSION
20 sts and 28 rows to 10 cm/4 in square over st st on 4 mm (No 8/US 5) needles.

## ABBREVIATIONS
See page 5.

## NOTE
Read Charts from right to left on right side rows and from left to right on wrong side rows. When working in pattern, use separate small balls of yarn for each coloured area and twist yarns together on wrong side when changing colour to avoid holes.

## BACK
With 3¼ mm (No 10/US 3) needles and MC, cast on 70(78:82) sts.
**1st row** (right side) K2, [P2, K2] to end.
**2nd row** P2, [K2, P2] to end.
Rep last 2 rows until work measures 4 cm/1½ in from beg, ending with a 2nd row and inc 2 sts evenly across last row on **1st** and **3rd** sizes only. 72(78:84) sts.
Change to 4 mm (No 8/US 5) needles.
Beg with a K row, work 4(6:10) rows in st st.
Place Chart 1 as follows:
**Next row** K32(35:38)MC, K across 1st row of Chart 1, K2(5:8)MC.
**Next row** P2(5:8)MC, P across 2nd row of Chart 1, P32(35:38)MC.
Cont working from Chart as set, work a further 6 rows.
Place Chart 2 as follows:
**Next row** K2(2:5)MC, K across 1st row of Chart 2, K4(7:7)MC, K across 9th row of Chart 1, K2(5:8) MC.
**Next row** P2(5:8)MC, P across 10th row of Chart 1, P4(7:7)MC, P across 2nd row of Chart 2, P2(2:5)MC.
Cont working from Charts as set, work a further 30 rows, working sts in MC when Chart 2 has been completed.
With MC only, work 10(12:14) rows in st st.
Place Chart 3 as follows:
**Next row** K3MC, K across 1st row of Chart 3, K39(45:51)MC.
**Next row** P39(45:51)MC, P across 2nd row of Chart 3, P3MC.
Cont working from Chart as set, work a further 6 rows.
Place Chart 4 as follows:
**Next row** K3MC, K across 9th row of Chart 3, K8(11:14)MC, K across 1st row

of Chart 4, K4(7:10)MC.
**Next row** P4(7:10)MC, P across 2nd row of Chart 4, P8(11:14)MC, P across 10th row of Chart 3, P3MC.
Cont working from Charts as set, work a further 28 rows, working sts in MC when Chart 4 has been completed.

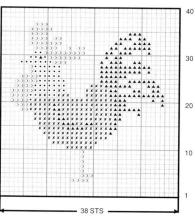

CHART 1

40

30

20

10

1

38 STS

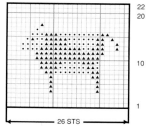

CHART 2

22
20

10

1

26 STS

Cont in st st and MC only until work measures 44(47:50) cm/17¼(18½:19¾) in from beg, ending with a P row.
### Shape Shoulders
Cast off 23(26:28) sts at beg of next 2 rows. Leave rem 26(26:28) sts on a holder.

## FRONT
Work as given for Back until Front measures 39(41:44) cm/15¼(16:17¼) in from beg, ending with a P row.
### Shape Neck
**Next row** K30(33:35), turn.
Work on this set of sts only. Dec one st at neck edge on every row until 23(26:28) sts rem. Cont straight until Front matches Back to shoulders, ending at side edge. Cast off.
With right side facing, slip centre 12(12:14) sts onto a holder, rejoin yarn to rem sts and K to end. Complete to match first side.

## SLEEVES
With 3¼mm (No 10/US 3) needles and MC, cast on 38(38:42) sts.
Work 4 cm/1½ in in rib as given for Back welt, ending with a 1st row.
**Inc row** Rib 5(4:3), inc in next st, [rib 8(5:6), inc in next st] to last 5(3:3) sts, rib 5(3:3). 42(44:48) sts.
Change to 4 mm (No 8/US 5) needles.
Beg with a K row, work 4(4:6) rows in st st.
Place Chart 2 as follows:

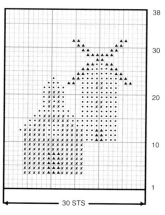

CHART 3

38

30

20

10

1

30 STS

## KEY
☐ = Blue
• = Cream
▲ = Rust
○ = Red
× = Brown
✎ = Pink

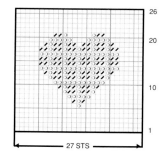

CHART 4

26

20

10

1

27 STS

**Next row** With MC, K twice in first st, K5(6:8), K across 1st row of Chart 2, with MC, K to last st, K twice in last st.
**Next row** P11(12:14)MC, P across 2nd row of Chart 2, with MC, P to end.
Cont working from Chart as set until 22nd row of Chart 2 has been worked, **at the same time**, inc one st at each end of 3rd row and every foll 4th row, working inc sts in MC. 54(56:60) sts.
With MC only, work 10(12:14) rows in st st, inc one st at each end of 3rd row and 1(2:2) foll 4th rows. 58(62:66) sts.
Place Chart 4 as follows:
**Next row** K18(20:22)MC, K across 1st

row of Chart 4, K13(15:17)MC.
**Next row** P13(15:17)MC, P across 2nd row of Chart 4, P18(20:22)MC.
Cont working from Chart as set until 26th row of Chart 4 has been worked, **at the same time**, inc one st at each end of next row and 1(1:2) foll 6th rows, working inc sts in MC. 62(66:72) sts.
Cont in MC only, work 4(6:8) rows in st st. Cast off.

### NECKBAND
Join right shoulder seam.
With 3¼ mm (No 10/US 3) needles, MC and right side facing, pick up and K

16(18:18) sts down left front neck, K centre front sts, pick up and K16 (18:18) sts up right front neck, K back neck sts. 70(74:78) sts.
Beg with a 2nd row, work 7 cm/2¾ in in rib as given for Back welt. Cast off loosely in rib.

### TO MAKE UP
Join left shoulder and neckband seam.
Sew on sleeves, placing centre of sleeves to shoulder seams.
Join side and sleeve seams. With Rust, embroider stitching around each motif rectangle.

# *Knitted Toys*

See Page
## 24

---

### MATERIALS
**Cat** 1×50 g ball of Rowan Designer DK Wool.
Oddment of White for embroidery.
**Lamb** 1×50 g ball of Rowan Designer DK Wool in Cream (A).
Small amount of same in Black.
**Pig** 1×50 g ball of Rowan Designer DK Wool.
Oddment of Black for embroidery.

Medium size crochet hook.

Pair of 3¾ mm (No 9/US 4) knitting needles.
Kapok for stuffing.
4 pipe cleaners.
Length of ribbon.

### ABBREVIATIONS
See page 5.

## CAT

### BODY AND LEGS
Cast on 40 sts. Cont in st st until work is a square. Cast off.

### HEAD
Cast on 5 sts. P 1 row.
**1st row** (right side) K twice in first st, [K1, m1] twice, K1, K twice in last st.
**2nd row** P twice in first st, P to last st, P twice in last st.
**3rd row** K twice in first st, K4, m1, K1, m1, K4, K twice in last st.
**4th row** As 2nd row.
**5th row** K twice in first st, K7, m1, K1, m1, K7, K twice in last st. 21 sts.
Work 3 rows in st st.
**9th row** K8, K2 tog, K1, sl 1, K1, psso, K8.
**10th row** P.
**11th row** K7, K2 tog, K1, sl 1, K1, psso, K7. 17 sts.
Work 7 rows in st st.
Dec one st at each end of next 4 rows. 9 sts. K 1 row.
Inc one st at each end of next 4 rows. 17 sts. Work 13 rows in st st.
Dec one st at each end of next 6 rows. 5 sts. Cast off.

### EARS (make 2)
Cast on 4 sts. K 1 row.
**Next row** K1, [m1, K1] 3 times. 7 sts.
K 3 rows.
**Next row** Sl 1, K1, psso, K3, K2 tog.
K 1 row.

**Next row** Sl 1, K1, psso, K1, K2 tog.
K 1 row. K3 tog and fasten off.

### TAIL
Cast on 12 sts. Work 5 rows in st st. Cast off.

### TO MAKE UP
Join each of the 4 corners of body and leg pieces together for approximately 6 cm/2¼ in to form legs. Twist together 2 pairs of pipe cleaners and bend them in half. Insert ends of one pair of pipe cleaners in back legs and other in front legs. Stuff and join opening. Wrap tightly a length of yarn twice around each leg approximately 3 cm/1¼ in from lower edge and secure. Fold head piece in half widthwise and join side seams. Stuff firmly and sew to body. ** Fold cast on edge of ears in half and stitch together, then sew them in place. With P side on the outside, join cast on and cast off edges of tail together and attach to body. With White, embroider eyes. Place ribbon around cat's neck and tie into a bow.

## LAMB

### BODY AND LEGS
Cast on 40 sts. Cont in garter st (every row K) until work measures a square. Cast off.

### HEAD, EARS AND TAIL
With Black, work as given for Head, Ears and Tail of Cat.

### TO MAKE UP
Work as given for To Make Up of Cat.

## PIG

### BODY AND LEGS
Work as given for Body and Legs of Lamb.

### HEAD
Cast on 7 sts. Work in garter st, inc one st at each end of next 5 rows. 17 sts. K 14 rows straight. Dec one st at each end of next 3 rows. K 2 rows.
Inc one st at each end of next 3 rows. 17 sts. K 14 rows straight.
Dec one st at each end of next 5 rows. 7 sts. Cast off.

### SNOUT
Cast on 4 sts for outside. K 18 rows. Cast off.
Cast on 3 sts for centre. K 1 row. Cont in garter st, inc one st at each end of next row. K 2 rows. Dec one st at each end of next row. K 1 row. Cast off.

### EARS (make 2)
Cast on 3 sts. K 1 row. Cont in garter st, inc one st at each end of next row and foll alt row. K 6 rows. Dec one st at each end of next row and foll alt row. Break off yarn, thread end through rem sts, pull up and secure.

### TO MAKE UP
Work as given for To Make Up of Cat to **. Join cast on and cast off edges of outside of snout together. Sew in centre at one end. Stuff and sew other end to head. Sew on ears. With Black, embroider eyes and nostrils. Place ribbon around pig's neck and tie into a bow. Using a crochet hook and 2 strands of yarn together, work a chain approximately 6 cm/2¼ in long for tail. Fasten off and attach to body.

# *Sheep*

See Page
## 24

## MEASUREMENTS
Approximate height 23 cm/9 in.

## MATERIALS
3×50 g balls of Rowan Designer DK Wool in Cream (MC).
1×50 g ball of same in Black (A).
Small amount of same in Brown.
Pair of 3¼ mm (No 10/US 3) knitting needles.
Stuffing.

## TENSION
26 sts and 50 rows to 10 cm/4 in square over garter st (every row K).

## ABBREVIATIONS
See page 5.

## UPPER BODY
With MC, cast on 58 sts. K1 row. Mark centre of last row. Cont in garter st.
### Shape Back Legs
Cast on 6 sts at beg of next 4 rows and 3 sts at beg of foll 2 rows. 88 sts.
Work 20 rows straight. Cast off 3 sts at beg of next 2 rows. Dec one st at each end of next row, 2 foll alt rows, then on foll 3 rows. 70 sts.
Inc one st at each end of 7th row and 2 foll 6th rows. 76 sts.
Work 29 rows straight. Dec one st at each end of next row and 2 foll 6th rows. 70 sts.
Work 7 rows straight.
### Shape Front Legs
Cast on 3 sts at beg of next 6 rows. 88 sts. Work 20 rows straight. Cast off 3 sts at beg of next 4 rows. Dec one st at each end of next row and 5 foll alt rows, then on every row until 38 sts rem. Work 3 rows. Cast off.

## UNDERSIDE
With MC, cast on 5 sts. Mark centre st of cast on row. Work in garter st, inc one st at each end of 3rd row, foll alt row and 3 foll 8th rows. 15 sts.
Work 9 rows straight.
### Shape Back Legs
Cast on 6 sts at beg of next 4 rows and 3 sts at beg of foll 2 rows. 45 sts.
Work 1 row.
**Next row** K15, K2 tog tbl, K11, K2 tog, K15.
Work 3 rows.
**Next row** K14, K2 tog tbl, K11, K2 tog, K14.
Cont in this way, dec 2 sts as set on every foll 4th row until 35 sts rem.

Work 2 rows. Cast off 3 sts at beg of next row.
**Next row** Cast off 3 sts, K6 sts more, K2 tog tbl, K11, K2 tog, K to end.
Dec one st at each end of next row and 2 foll alt rows, then on foll 3 rows. 15 sts.
Inc one st at each end of 7th row and 2 foll 6th rows. 21 sts. Work 29 rows straight. Dec one st at each end of next row and 2 foll 6th rows. 15 sts.
Work 7 rows straight.
### Shape Front Legs
Cast on 3 sts at beg of next 6 rows. 33 sts. Work 20 rows straight. Cast off 3 sts at beg of next 4 rows. Dec one st at each end of next row and every foll 6th row until 9 sts rem. Work 3 rows straight. Cast off.

## HEAD
With A, cast on 47 sts.
**Next row** K37, turn.
**Next row** P27, turn.
**Next row** K23, turn.
**Next row** P19, turn.
**Next row** K15, turn.
**Next row** P11, turn.
**Next row** K to end.
Beg with a P row, work 5 rows in st st.
**Next row** K7, K2 tog, K6, K2 tog tbl, K13, K2 tog, K6, K2 tog tbl, K7.
**Next row** P14, P2 tog, P11, P2 tog tbl, P14.
**Next row** K6, K2 tog, K6, K2 tog tbl, K9, K2 tog, K6, K2 tog tbl, K6.
**Next row** P13, P2 tog, P7, P2 tog tbl, P13.
**Next row** K5, [K2 tog, K6, K2 tog tbl, K5] twice.
P 1 row.
**Next row** K4, K2 tog, K6, K2 tog tbl, K3, K2 tog, K6, K2 tog tbl, K4.
Work 3 rows in st st.
**Next row** K10, K2 tog, K3, K2 tog tbl, K10.
Work 9 rows in st st, dec one st at centre of 7th row. 24 sts.
### Shape Muzzle
**Next row** K3, cast off 6, K5 sts more, cast off 6, K to end.
Work 3 rows on last set of 3 sts. Leave these sts on a holder. With wrong side facing, rejoin yarn to centre 6 sts and work 3 rows. Leave these sts on a holder. With wrong side facing, rejoin yarn to rem 3 sts and work 3 rows.
Slip these 3 sts and last 3 sts onto one needle. Place these sts to centre 6 sts with right sides together, then cast them off together.

## FEET (make 8)
With A, cast on 14 sts. Work 14 rows in st st. Cast off.

## HORNS (make 2)
With Brown, cast on 12 sts. P1 row. K1 row. P2 rows. These 4 rows form patt. Cont in patt, work 6 rows. Dec one st at each end of next row and every foll 4th row until 2 sts rem, ending with a wrong side row. P2 tog and fasten off.

## EARS (make 2)
With MC, cast on 6 sts. Work in garter st, dec one st at each end of 5th row and foll alt row. Work 1 row. K2 tog and fasten off.

## TO MAKE UP
Join upper body to underside, matching marker and legs and leaving row ends of legs free. Fold first 2 sts of row ends of legs to inside and slip stitch in place. Join paired pieces of feet together, leaving one row end edge open. Place feet inside legs and sew in position. Fold last 2 rows of cast off edge of body and underside to inside and slip stitch in place. Join head seam. Place cast off seam of muzzle at centre, then join row ends to cast off sts. Stuff body and head. Sew head to body. Roll horns widthwise and slip stitch top edge, then pull thread, thus curling the horns. Sew horns and ears in place. With MC, embroider eyes.

# *Cow*

See Page
## *24*

## MEASUREMENTS

Approximate height 23 cm/9 in.

## MATERIALS
3 × 50 g balls of Rowan Designer DK
Wool in Cream (MC).
1 × 50 g ball of same in Black (A).
Small amount of same in each of Pink,
Brown and Rust.
Pair of 3¼ mm (No 10/US 3) knitting
needles.
Stuffing.

## TENSION
26 sts and 50 rows to 10 cm/4 in
square over garter st (every row K).

## ABBREVIATIONS
See page 5.

## NOTE
When working in pattern, use
separate small balls of yarn for each
coloured area and twist yarns together
on wrong side when changing colour
to avoid holes.

## UPPER BODY
### Left Back Leg
With MC, cast on 20 sts. K 1 row. Cont in
garter st, inc one st at beg of next row
and at same edge on every row until there
are 31 sts. K1 row. Leave these sts on a
holder.
### Right Back Leg
With MC, cast on 20 sts. K1 row. Cont in
garter st, inc one st at end of next row
and at same edge on every row until there
are 31 sts. K1 row.
### Shape Body
Next row (right side) K across sts of
Right Back Leg, cast on 58 sts, K across
sts of Left Back Leg. 120 sts. Mark centre
of last row.
K 3 rows. Cast off 13 sts at beg of next 2
rows. Dec one st at each end of next row
and 3 foll alt rows. 86 sts. K 1 row.
Place Chart 1 as follows:
Next row With MC, K2 tog, K14, reading
Chart 1 from right to left, K across 1st row,
K8MC, reading Chart 1 from left to right, K
across 1st row, with MC, K14, K2 tog.
Next row K15MC, reading Chart 1 from
right to left, K across 2nd row, K8MC,
reading Chart 1 from left to right, K across
2nd row, K15MC.
Cont working from Chart 1 as set, dec
one st at each end of next row and 3 foll

alt rows, then at each end of foll 2 rows.
72 sts. Patt 11 rows straight.
Now inc one st at each end of next row
and 2 foll alt rows then on foll 4th row. 80
sts. Patt 1 row.
Place Chart 2 as follows:
Next row Reading Chart 2 from right to
left, K across 1st row, patt to last 10 sts,
reading Chart 2 from left to right, K across
1st row.
Cont working from Charts as set, inc one
st at each end of 2nd row and foll 4th row,
working inc sts in A. 84 sts.
Patt 21 rows straight, working sts in MC
when Chart 1 has been completed.
Dec one st at each end of next row and 3
foll 4th rows. 76 sts. Patt 1 row.
Place Chart 3 as follows:
Next row Patt 11, reading Chart 3 from
right to left, K across 1st row, reading
Chart 3 from left to right, K across 1st row,
patt 11.
Cont working from Charts as set, patt 3
rows, thus completing Chart 2.
### Shape Front Legs
Cast on 4 sts at beg of next 6 rows and 10
sts at beg of foll 2 rows. 120 sts.
Patt 14 rows straight. Cast off 22 sts at
beg of next 2 rows. 76 sts.
Dec one st at each end of 5th row and
every foll alt row until 52 sts rem.

Patt 1 row. Cast off 2 sts at beg of next 2
rows. 48 sts. Patt 1 row.
Mark each end of last row.
### Shape Head
Next row Patt 16, cast off 16, patt 16.
Work on last set of 16 sts only for right
side of head. Inc one st at beg of next row
and 3 foll alt rows, **at the same time**, cast
off 2 sts at beg of 4 foll alt rows. 12 sts.
Cont in MC only. Dec one st at end of 3rd
row, then at each end of 3 foll 4th rows. K
2 rows. Mark each end of last row.
Inc one st at beg of next row. K 1 row.
Cast off.
With right side of work facing, rejoin yarn
to rem sts for left side of head and
complete to match right side, reversing
shaping.

## UNDERSIDE
With MC, cast on 3 sts. Mark centre st.
Work in garter st, inc one st at each end
of 3rd row, foll 6th row, foll 8th row, then
foll 10th row and foll 14th row. 13 sts. K 5
rows. Leave these sts on a holder.
### Left Back Leg
Work as for Left Back Leg of Upper Body.
### Right Back Leg
Work as for Right Back Leg of Upper
Body.
Next row K across sts of Right Back Leg,
K13 sts from holder, K across sts of Left
Back Leg. 75 sts.
K 3 rows. Cast off 13 sts at beg of next 2
rows. 49 sts.
Next row K2 tog, K16, K2 tog tbl, K9, K2
tog, K16, K2 tog.
K 1 row.
Next row K2 tog, K14, K2 tog tbl, K9, K2
tog, K14, K2 tog.
K 1 row.
Next row K2 tog, K12, K2 tog tbl, K9, K2
tog, K12, K2 tog. Cont in this way, dec 4
sts as set on every alt row until 21 sts rem.
Dec one st at each end of 2 foll alt rows,
then at each end of next 2 rows. 13 sts.
Inc one st at each end of 4 foll 6th rows.
21 sts. K 27 rows straight.
Dec one st at each end of next row and 3
foll 4th rows. 13 sts. K 3 rows.

CHART 1

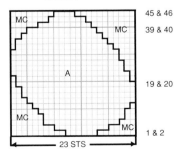

45 & 46
39 & 40

19 & 20

1 & 2

← 23 STS →

CHART 2

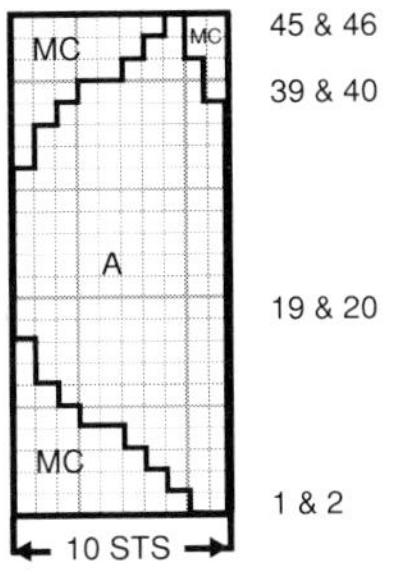

45 & 46
39 & 40

19 & 20

1 & 2

← 10 STS →

CHART 3

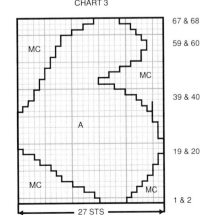

67 & 68

59 & 60

39 & 40

19 & 20

1 & 2

← 27 STS →

KEY

☐ = 1 ST AND
2 ROWS

### Shape Front Legs

Cast on 4 sts at beg of next 6 rows and 10 sts at beg of foll 2 rows. 57 sts.
K 14 rows. Cast off 22 sts at beg of next 2 rows. 13 sts.
Dec one st at each end of 7th row and 3 foll 6th rows. 5 sts. K 9 rows straight. Mark each end of last row.
Inc one st at each end of next row and foll alt row, then on 2 foll 4th rows. 13 sts.
Dec one st at each end of 2 foll 4th rows. K 3 rows.
Cast off 2 sts at beg of next 2 rows. 5 sts. K 2 rows. Mark each end of last row. Inc one st at each end of next row. 7 sts. K 13 rows.
Dec one st at each end of next row. 5 sts. Mark each end of last row.
Inc one st at each end of 6 foll 4th rows. 17 sts. K 5 rows. Cast off.

### UDDER

With MC, cast on 46 sts.
**Next 2 rows** K3, turn, P to end.
**Next 2 rows** K6, turn, P to end.
**Next 2 rows** K10, turn, P to end.
**Next 2 rows** K16, turn, P to end.
**Next row** K to end.
**Next 2 rows** P3, turn, K to end.
**Next 2 rows** P6, turn, K to end.
**Next 2 rows** P10, turn, K to end.
**Next 2 rows** P16, turn, K to end.
Beg with a P row, work 7 rows in st st.
**Next row** K1, [K2 tog, K3] to end.
Work 3 rows straight.
**Next row** K1, [K2 tog, K2] to end.
Work 1 row.
**Next row** K1, [K2 tog, K1] to end.
Work 1 row.
**Next row** K1, [K2 tog] to end. 10 sts.
Break off yarn, thread end through rem sts, pull up and secure.

### TEATS (make 4)

With Pink, cast on 5 sts. Beg with a K row, work 6 rows in st st.
**Next row** K1, [K2 tog] twice.
Break off yarn, thread end through rem sts, pull up and secure.

### EARS (make 2)

With MC, cast on 5 sts. K 10 rows. Dec one st at each end of next row.
K3 tog and fasten off.

### HORNS (make 2)

With Brown, cast on 4 sts. Beg with a K row, work 4 rows in st st.
**Next row** [K2 tog] twice.
Break off yarn, thread end through rem sts, pull up and secure.

### TAIL

With MC, cast on 30 sts. Cast off.

### TO MAKE UP

Join upper body to underside, matching legs and markers and leaving an opening. Stuff firmly and close opening. Join back seam of udder, stuff lightly and sew in place. Join seam of teats and sew in place. Join seam of horns and sew in position. Sew on ears. With MC, work fringe along top of head. With Rust, embroider eyes. Make small tassel with MC and attach to one end of tail. Attach other end to body.

# *Pig*

See Page
## 24

### MEASUREMENTS

Approximate height 23 cm/9 in.

### MATERIALS

3 × 50 g balls of Rowan Designer DK Wool.
Oddment of Black for embroidery.
Pair of 3¼ mm (No 10/US 3) knitting needles.
Stuffing.

### TENSION

26 sts and 50 rows to 10 cm/4 in square over garter st (every row K).

### ABBREVIATIONS

See page 5.

### UPPER BODY

Cast on 76 sts. Mark centre and 6th sts from each end. K 1 row.
#### Shape Back Legs
Cont in garter st, cast on 6 sts at beg of next 4 rows and 12 sts at beg of foll 2 rows. 124 sts. K 22 rows. Cast off 12 sts at beg of next 2 rows and 6 sts at beg of foll 4 rows. 76 sts. K 66 rows.
#### Shape Front Legs
Cast on 24 sts at beg of next 2 rows. 124 sts. K 18 rows. Cast off 24 sts at beg of next 2 rows. 76 sts. K 19 rows.
#### Shape Head
**Next row** (wrong side) K16, [K2 tog tbl, K9] twice, [K9, K2 tog] twice, K16.
K 5 rows straight.
**Next row** K16, [K2 tog tbl, K8] twice, [K8, K2 tog] twice, K16.
K 5 rows straight. Mark each end of last row.
**Next row** K16, [K2 tog tbl, K7] twice, [K7, K2 tog] twice, K16.
Cont in this way, dec 4 sts as set on 2 foll alt rows and 3 foll 4th rows. 44 sts. K 14 rows.

**Next row** K6, [K twice in next st, K5] 6 times, K2. 50 sts.
K 3 rows. Cast off.

### UNDERSIDE

Cast on 3 sts. Mark centre st. K 1 row.
Cont in garter st, inc one st at each end of next 3 rows and 4 foll alt rows. 17 sts. K 13 rows straight. Dec one st at each end of next row and 2 foll 4th rows. 11 sts. K 7 rows straight. Mark each end of last row.
#### Shape Back Legs
Cast on 6 sts at beg of next 6 rows and 12 sts at beg of foll 2 rows. 71 sts.
**Next row** K30, K2 tog tbl, K7, K2 tog, K30.
K 5 rows straight.
**Next row** K29, K2 tog tbl, K7, K2 tog, K29.
K 5 rows straight.
**Next row** K28, K2 tog tbl, K7, K2 tog, K28.
K 5 rows straight.
**Next row** K27, K2 tog tbl, K7, K2 tog, K27.
K 3 rows straight. Cast off 12 sts at beg of

next 2 rows.
**Next row** Cast off 6 sts, K until there are 8 sts on right-hand needle, K2 tog tbl, K7, K2 tog, K14.
Cast off 6 sts at beg of next 3 rows. 13 sts. K 66 rows.
#### Shape Front Legs
Cast on 24 sts at beg of next 2 rows. 61 sts. K 18 rows. Cast off 24 sts at beg of next 2 rows. 13 sts. K 8 rows.
Dec one st at each end of next row and 4 foll 4th rows. 3 sts. K 1 row.
K3 tog and fasten off.

### SNOUT

Cast on 3 sts. K 1 row. Cont in garter st, inc one st at each end of next 3 rows and 3 foll alt rows. 15 sts. K 7 rows. Dec one st at each end of next row and 2 foll alt rows, then on 3 foll rows. 3 sts. K 1 row. Cast off.

### EARS (make 2)

Cast on 17 sts. K 6 rows. Dec one st at each end of next row, 2 foll 4th rows, then 4 foll alt rows. 3 sts. K 1 row. K3 tog and fasten off.

### TAIL

Cast on loosely 20 sts. Cast off tightly.

### TO MAKE UP

Join seam from cast off edge to first marker. Sew in snout. Join upper body to underside, matching legs and markers and leaving an opening. Stuff firmly and close opening. Fold sides of each ear to centre at cast on edge and secure. Sew on ears and tail. With Black, embroider eyes, nostrils and mouth.

# Farmhouse with Cow and Sheep See Page 6

## MATERIALS

**Farmhouse** 1×50 g ball of Rowan DK Handknit Cotton in each of Blue (A) and Rust (B).
Small amount of same in each of Cream (C) and Brown (D).
Block of foam 11 cm×7 cm×12 cm/4¼ in×3¾ in×4¾ in.
**Cow** Small amount of Rowan DK Handknit Cotton in each of Cream (A) and Rust (B).
Oddment of same in Brown and Black.

Medium size crochet hook.
Wadding for stuffing.
**Sheep** Small amount of Rowan DK Handknit Cotton in each of Cream (A) and Black (B).
Wadding for stuffing.

Pair of 3¼ mm (No 10/US 3) knitting needles.

## ABBREVIATIONS
See page 5.

## FARMHOUSE

### FRONT WALL, ROOF AND BACK WALL
With A, cast on 26 sts. Beg with a K row, work 30 rows in st st.
Change to B and K 46 rows. Change to A and beg with a K row, work 30 rows in st st. Cast off.

### SIDE WALLS (make 2)
With B, cast on 18 sts. Work 20 rows in st st. Dec one st at each end of next row and every foll alt row until 4 sts rem. Cast off.

### FRONT WINDOWS (make 2)
With C, cast on 8 sts. K 8 rows. Cast off.

### SIDE WINDOW
With D, cast on 6 sts. K 8 rows. Cast off.

### SIDE DOOR
With D, cast on 10 sts. K 20 rows. Cast off.

### TO MAKE UP
Leaving first 10 rows of front wall and last 10 rows of back wall free, sew in side walls. Sew windows and door in place. Cut block of foam into house shape and insert into knitted house. Fold over the free ends of walls and join together cast on and cast off edge, then join sides to side walls.

## COW

### BODY AND HEAD
With 3¼ mm (No 10/US 3) needles and A, cast on 28 sts. Work in garter st (every row K) for 32 rows.
**Next row** K2 tog tbl, K5, K2 tog, K10, K2 tog tbl, K5, K2 tog.
Dec one st at each end of every alt row until 16 sts rem.
Shape Head
**Next row** K11, turn.
**Next row** K6, turn.
**Next row** K5, turn.
**Next row** K4, turn.
**Next row** K2, turn.
**Next row** K3, turn.
**Next row** K to end.
Dec one st at each end of next row. 14 sts.
**Next row** [K2 tog] to end.
Break off yarn, thread end through rem sts, pull up and secure.

### LEGS (make 4)
With 3¼ mm (No 10/US 3) needles and A, cast on 10 sts. K 10 rows. Cast off.

### LARGE SPOT
With 3¼ mm (No 10/US 3) needles and B, cast on 5 sts. K 1 row. Cont in garter st, inc one st at each end of next row and foll alt row. 9 sts. K 8 rows. Dec one st at each end of next row and foll alt row. K 1 row. Cast off.

### SMALL SPOTS (make 2)
With 3¼ mm (No 10/US 3) needles and B, cast on 3 sts. K 1 row. Cont in garter st, inc one st at each end of next row and foll alt row. 7 sts. K 2 rows. Dec one st at each end of next row and foll alt row. K 1 row. Cast off.

### EARS (make 2)
With 3¼ mm (No 10/US 3) needles and A, cast on 5 sts. K 2 rows. Dec one st at each end of next row. K 1 row. K 3 tog and fasten off.

### TO MAKE UP
Join underside seam of body, leaving cast on edge open. Stuff and close opening. Join cast on and cast off edges of legs together. Gather one end, pull up and secure. Stuff legs and attach to body. Sew large spot on back of body and small spots at sides. With crochet hook and B, make a chain 4 cm/1½ in long for tail. Make small tassel at one end of tail, attach other end to body. With crochet hook and Brown, make a chain 4 cm/1½ in long for horns. Place horns on top of head and over sew centre of them with A. Sew on ears. With Black, embroider eyes and nostrils.

## SHEEP

### BODY AND HEAD
With A, cast on 20 sts. K 19 rows. Dec one st at each end of next row and 2 foll alt rows. 14 sts. Change to B. Beg with a K row, work 8 rows in st st. Break off yarn, thread end through rem sts, pull up and secure.

### LEGS (make 4)
With B, cast on 7 sts. Work 8 rows in st st. Cast off.

### EARS (make 2)
With B, cast on 5 sts. K 2 rows. Dec one st at each end of next row. K 1 row. K3 tog and fasten off.

### TAIL
With B, cast on 4 sts. Work 4 rows in st st. Cast off.

### TO MAKE UP
Join underside seam of body, leaving cast on edge open. Stuff and close opening. Join cast on and cast off edges of legs together. Gather one end, pull up and secure. Stuff legs and attach to body. Fold tail lengthwise and join seam all round. Sew tail and ears in place. With A, embroider eyes. Add small Black dot at centre of each eye for pupils.

# Farmyard Jacket

See Page
## 26

## MEASUREMENTS

| To fit age | 2 | 3 | Years |
|---|---|---|---|
| Actual chest measurement | 74 | 79 | cm |
| | 29 | 31 | in |
| Length | 31 | 34 | cm |
| | 12¼ | 13½ | in |
| Sleeve seam | 23 | 26 | cm |
| | 9 | 10¼ | in |

## MATERIALS
5(6) 50 g balls of Rowan Designer DK Wool in Green (MC).
1(1) 50 g ball of same in each of Brown, Yellow, Cream, Black, Blue, Red and Pink.
Pair each of 3¼ mm (No 10/US 3) and 4 mm (No 8/US 5) knitting needles.
5 buttons.

## TENSION
24 sts and 32 rows to 10 cm/4 in square over st st on 4 mm (No 8/US 5) needles.

## ABBREVIATIONS
See page 5.

## NOTE
Read Chart from right to left on right side rows and from left to right on wrong side rows. When working in pattern, use separate lengths of yarn for each coloured area and twist yarns together on wrong side when changing colour to avoid holes.

## BACK
With 3¼ mm (No 10/US 3) needles and MC, cast on 87(93) sts.
**1st row** (right side)  K1, [P1, K1] to end.
**2nd row**  P1, [K1, P1] to end.
Rep last 2 rows until work measures 4(5) cm/1½ (2) in from beg, ending with a 2nd row.
Change to 4 mm (No 8/US 5) needles.
Beg with a K row, cont in st st throughout, work 4(8) rows.
Now work patt from Chart until 70th row of Chart has been worked.
Cont in MC only, work 14 rows.
### Shape Shoulders
Cast off 14(16) sts at beg of next 2 rows and 15 sts at beg of foll 2 rows.
Leave rem 29(31) sts on a holder.

## LEFT FRONT
With 3¼ mm (No 10/US 3) needles and MC, cast on 43(45) sts.
Work 4(5) cm/1½(2) in in rib as given for Back welt, ending with a 2nd row and inc one st at centre of last row on **2nd** size only. 43(46) sts.
Change to 4 mm (No 8/US 5) needles.
Beg with a K row, cont in st st throughout, work 4(8) rows.
Now work patt from Chart until 58th row of Chart has been worked.
### Shape Neck
Keeping patt correct, dec one st at front edge on every row until 70th row of Chart has been worked.
Cont in MC only, work 2(3) rows, dec one st at front edge of every row. 29(31) sts.
Work 12(11) rows straight.
### Shape Shoulder
Cast off 14(16) sts at beg of next row.
Work 1 row. Cast off rem 15 sts.
### RIGHT FRONT
Work to match Left Front, reversing shoulder shaping.

## SLEEVES
With 3¼ mm (No 10/US 3) needles and MC, cast on 43(45) sts.

Work 4(5) cm/1½(2) in in rib as given for Back welt, ending with a 2nd row and inc 2 sts evenly across last row. 45(47) sts.
Change to 4 mm (No 8/US 5) needles.
Beg with a K row, cont in st st throughout, work 4(8) rows, inc one st at each end of 0(5th) row. 45(49) sts.
Now work patt from Chart until 52nd row of Chart has been worked, **at the same time**, inc one st at each end of 3rd row and every foll 4th row until there are 69(73) sts, working inc sts into patt. Cont in MC only, work 4(8) rows. Cast off.

## FRONT BANDS AND COLLAR
Join shoulder seams.
With 3¼ mm (No 10/US 3) needles, MC and right side facing, pick up and K 55 (61) sts along straight edge of Right Front, 38 sts along shaped edge to shoulder, K back neck sts inc 8 sts evenly, pick up and K 38 sts down shaped edge of Left Front and 55(61) sts along straight edge. 223(237) sts.
Beg with a 2nd row, work 3 rows in rib as given for Back welt.
**1st buttonhole row**  Rib 3, [cast off 2, rib 9(11) sts more] 5 times, rib to end.
**2nd buttonhole row**  Rib to end, casting on 2 sts over those cast off in previous row.
**Next 2 rows**  Rib to last 55(61) sts, turn, sl 1, rib to last 55(61) sts, turn.
**Next 2 rows**  Sl 1, rib to last 57(63) sts, turn.
**Next 2 rows**  Sl 1, rib to last 59(65) sts, turn.
Cont in this way, working 2 sts less at end of every row on next 12(14) rows.
**Next row**  Rib to end.
Rib 2 rows. Cast off in rib.

## TO MAKE UP
Sew on sleeves, placing centre of sleeves to shoulder seams. Join side and sleeve seams. Sew on buttons. Embroider eyes with Black and moustache with Brown on each farmer's face. With Black, embroider scarecrow's eyes and nose and with Yellow embroider straw hands. Sew small dot in Black on each cockerel's eye and with Yellow embroider beak and back claw.

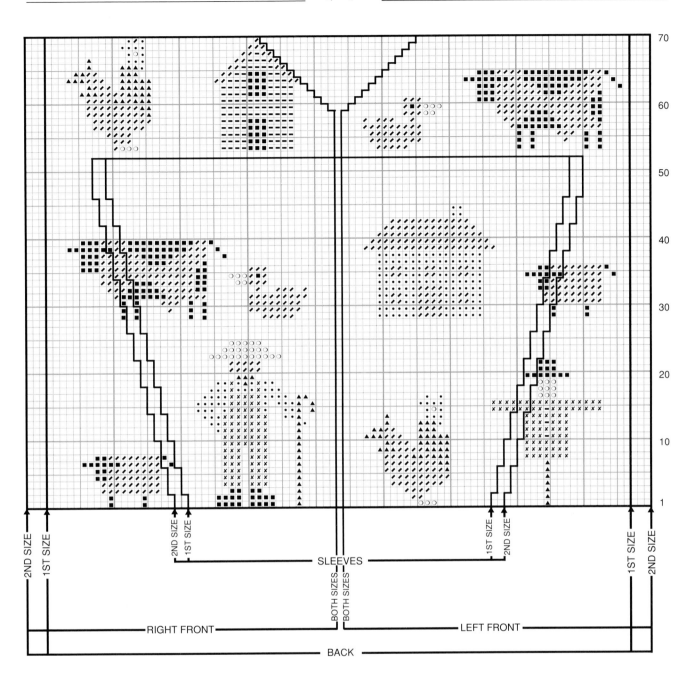

70

60

50

40

30

20

10

1

2ND SIZE

1ST SIZE

2ND SIZE

1ST SIZE

SLEEVES

1ST SIZE

2ND SIZE

1ST SIZE

2ND SIZE

BOTH SIZES
BOTH SIZES

RIGHT FRONT

LEFT FRONT

BACK

KEY

☐ = Green     ■ = Black

▲ = Brown     ✗ = Blue

○ = Yellow     • = Red

✦ = Cream     ▬ = Pink

# Duck and Sheep Fairisle Cardigan

See Page
## 27

## MEASUREMENTS

| To fit age | 3–4 | 5–6 | Years |
|---|---|---|---|
| Actual chest measurement | 78 | 89 | **cm** |
| | 30¾ | 35 | **in** |
| Length to shoulder | 46 | 49 | **cm** |
| | 18 | 19¼ | **in** |
| Sleeve seam | 25 | 28 | **cm** |
| | 10 | 11 | **in** |

## MATERIALS
4(5) 50 g balls of Rowan DK Handknit Cotton in Navy (MC).
3(4) 50 g balls of same in Green (A).
2(2) 50 g balls of same in Cream (B).
1(2) 50 g balls of same in each of Rust (C) and Brown (D).
1(1) 50 g ball of same in Blue (E).
Pair each of 3¼ mm (No 10/US 3) and 4 mm (No 8/US 5) knitting needles.
One 3¼ mm (No 10/US 3) circular needle.
5 buttons.

## TENSION
22 sts and 24 rows to 10 cm/4 in square over patt on 4 mm (No 8/US 5) needles.

## ABBREVIATIONS
See page 5.

## NOTE
Read Chart from right to left on K rows and from left to right on P rows. Strand yarn not in use loosely across wrong side when working in pattern to keep fabric elastic.

## BACK
With 3¼ mm (No 10/US 3) needles and MC, cast on 78(90) sts.
**1st row** (right side) K2, [P2, K2] to end.
**2nd row** P2, [K2, P2] to end.
Rep these 2 rows until work measures 4 cm/1½ in from beg, ending with a right side row.
**Inc row** Rib 7(9), inc in next st, [rib 8(9), inc in next st] 7 times, rib 7(10). 86(98) sts.
Change to 4 mm (No 8/US 5) needles.
Beg with a K row, work in st st and patt from Chart as indicated for Back until Back measures 46(49) cm/18(19¼) in from beg, ending with a wrong side row.
### Shape Shoulders
Cast off 14(16) sts at beg of next 4 rows.
Leave rem 30(34) sts on a holder.

## LEFT FRONT
With 3¼ mm (No 10/US 3) needles and MC, cast on 38(42) sts.
Work 4 cm/1½ in in rib as on Back welt, ending with a right side row.
**Inc row** Rib 9(5), inc in next st, [rib 18(9), inc in next st] 1(3) times, rib 9(6). 40(46) sts.
Change to 4 mm (No 8/US 5) needles.
Beg with a K row, work in st st and patt from Chart as indicated for Left Front until Front measures 25(26) cm/10(10¼) in from beg, ending with a wrong side row.
### Shape Front
Dec one st at end (front edge) of next row and 1(3) foll alt rows then on every foll 4th row until 28(32) sts rem.

Cont straight until Front matches Back to shoulder shaping, ending with a wrong side row.
### Shape Shoulder
Cast off 14(16) sts at beg of next row.
Work 1 row. Cast off rem 14(16) sts.

## RIGHT FRONT
Work as for Left Front, working patt from Chart as indicated for Right Front and reversing shapings.

## SLEEVES
With 3¼ mm (No 10/US 3) needles and MC, cast on 38(42) sts.
Work 5 cm/2 in in rib as on Back welt, ending with a right side row.
**Inc row** Rib 3, inc in next st, [rib 5(6), inc in next st] 5 times, rib 4(3). 44(48) sts.
Change to 4 mm (No 8/US 5) needles.
Beg with a K row, work in st st and patt from Chart as indicated for Sleeves, **at the same time**, inc one st at each end of every foll 3rd row until there are 72(76) sts, working inc sts into patt.
Cont straight until Sleeve measures 25(28) cm/10 (11) in from beg, ending with a wrong side row. Cast off.

## FRONT BAND
Join shoulder seams.
With right side of work facing, 3¼ mm (No 10/US 3) circular needle and MC, pick up and K 52(54) sts up straight front edge of Right Front, 52(56) sts up shaped edge to shoulder, K across back neck sts dec 4 sts evenly, pick up and K 52(56) sts down

shaped edge of Left Front and 52(54) sts down straight front edge. 234(250) sts.
Beg with a 2nd row, work 3 rows in rib as on Back welt.
**1st buttonhole row** Rib 3(4), [cast off 2, rib 8 sts more] 5 times, rib to end.
**2nd buttonhole row** Rib to end casting on 2 sts over those cast off in previous row.
Rib 3 rows. Cast off in rib.

## TO MAKE UP
Sew on sleeves, placing centre of sleeves to shoulder seams. Join side and sleeve seams. Sew on buttons.

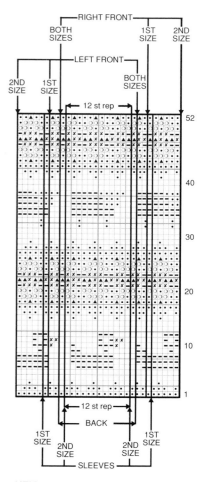

### KEY
- • = MC
- □ = A
- ▬ = B
- ✕ = C
- ○ = D
- ▲ = E

# Double Moss Stitch and Cable Jacket

See Page
## 28

## MEASUREMENTS

| To fit age | 2 | 3 | 4 | Years |
|---|---|---|---|---|
| Actual chest measurement | 76 | 80 | 83 | **cm** |
| | 30 | 31½ | 32¾ | **in** |
| Length to shoulder | 36 | 39 | 43 | **cm** |
| | 14¼ | 15½ | 17 | **in** |
| Sleeve seam (with cuff turned back) | 24 | 27 | 30 | **cm** |
| | 9½ | 10½ | 11¾ | **in** |

## MATERIALS
6(7:7) 50 g balls of Rowan Designer DK Wool in Red (MC).
1(1:1) 50 g ball of same in Black (A).
Small amount of same in each of Cream (B), Green (C), Pale Blue (D) and Gold (E).
Pair of 4 mm (No 8/US 5) knitting needles.
Medium size crochet hook.
Cable needle.
5 buttons.

## TENSION
26 sts and 34 rows to 10 cm/4 in square over double moss st patt on 4 mm (No 8/US 5) needles.

## ABBREVIATIONS
C4B = slip next 2 sts onto cable needle and leave at back of work, K2, then K2 from cable needle;
C4F = slip next 2 sts onto cable needle and leave at front of work, K2, then K2 from cable needle;
Cr3L = slip next 2 sts onto cable needle and leave at front of work, P1, then K2 from cable needle;
Cr3R = slip next st onto cable needle and leave at back of work, K2, then P1 from cable needle;
MB = make bobble, [K1, P1, K1, P1, K1, P1, K1] all in next st, then pass 2nd, 3rd, 4th, 5th, 6th and 7th st over first st;
ch = chain; dc = double crochet; ss = slip stitch.
Also see page 5.

## NOTE
Read Chart from right to left on right side rows and from left to right on wrong side rows. Use separate lengths of A, B, C, D and E yarn for each motif and twist yarns together on wrong side when changing colour to avoid holes. If preferred the motifs may be Swiss Darned when knitting is complete.

## CABLE PANEL – worked over 23 sts.
1st row (wrong side) P4, K5, P5, K5, P4.
2nd row K4, P5, K2, MB, K2, P5, K4.
3rd row As 1st row.
4th row C4B, P5, MB, K3, MB, P5, C4F.
5th row As 1st row.
6th row As 2nd row.
7th row As 1st row.
8th row C4B, P4, Cr3R, P1, Cr3L, P4, C4F.
9th row P4, K4, P2, K1, P1, K1, P2, K4, P4.
10th row K4, P3, Cr3R, K1, P1, K1, Cr3L, P3, K4.
11th row P4, K3, P3, K1, P1, K1, P3, K3, P4.
12th row C4B, P2, Cr3R, P1, [K1, P1] twice, Cr3L, P2, C4F.
13th row P4, K2, P2, K1, [P1, K1] 3 times, P2, K2, P4.
14th row K4, P2, K3, [P1, K1] 3 times, K2, P2, K4.
15th row As 13th row.
16th row C4B, P2, Cr3L, P1, [K1, P1] twice, Cr3R, P2, C4F.
17th row As 11th row.
18th row K4, P3, Cr3L, K1, P1, K1, Cr3R, P3, K4.
19th row As 9th row.
20th row C4B, P4, Cr3L, P1, Cr3R, P4, C4F.
These 20 rows form Cable Panel patt.

## RIGHT FRONT
With 4 mm (No 8/US 5) needles and MC, cast on 57(59:61) sts.
Work in patt as follows:
1st row (wrong side) With MC, [K1, P1] 6(7:8) times, K1, work 1st row of Cable Panel, K1, P2, P across 1st row of Chart, P6MC.
2nd row K6MC, K across 2nd row of Chart, with MC, K2, P1, work 2nd row of Cable Panel, P1, [K1, P1] 6(7:8) times.
3rd row With MC, [P1, K1] 6(7:8) times, K1, work 3rd row of Cable Panel, K1, P2, P across 3rd row of Chart, P6MC.
4th row K6MC, K across 4th row of Chart, with MC, K2, P1, work 4th row of Cable Panel, P1, [K1, P1] 6(7:8) times.

These 4 rows set position of Cable Panel and Chart and form double moss st at side edge. Cont in patt as set, working appropriate rows of Cable Panel and Chart until 17th(19th:23rd) row has been worked.
1st buttonhole row With MC, K2, cast off 2, patt to end.
2nd buttonhole row Patt to last 2 sts, with MC, cast on 2 sts, P2.
Patt 18(20:22) rows.
Rep last 20(22:24) rows 3 times more, then the 2 buttonhole rows again.
Patt 2 rows.
## Shape Neck
Cast off 9(10:11) sts at beg of next row and 3 sts at beg of 4 foll alt rows. Dec one st at neck edge on next 6 rows. Patt 2(4:6) rows. Cast off rem 30(31:32) sts.

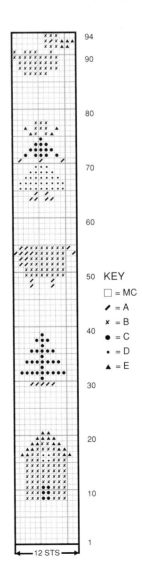

KEY
□ = MC
✦ = A
x = B
● = C
• = D
▲ = E

12 STS

## LEFT FRONT

With 4 mm (No 8/US 5) needles and MC, cast on 57(59:61) sts.
Work in patt as follows:
**1st row** (wrong side) P6MC, P across 1st row of Chart, with MC, P2, K1, work 1st row of Cable Panel, K1, [P1, K1] 6(7:8) times.
**2nd row** With MC, [P1, K1] 6(7:8) times, P1, work 2nd row of Cable Panel, P1, K2, K across 2nd row of Chart, K6MC.
**3rd row** P6MC, P across 3rd row of Chart, with MC, P2, K1, work 3rd row of Cable Panel, K1, [K1, P1] 6(7:8) times.
**4th row** With MC, [K1, P1] 6(7:8) times, P1, work 4th row of Cable Panel, P1, K2, K across 4th row of Chart, K6MC.
Complete to match Right Front, reversing shapings and omitting buttonholes.

## BACK

With 4 mm (No 8/US 5) needles and MC, cast on 97(101:107) sts.
Work in patt as follows:
**1st row** (wrong side) K1, [P1, K1] to end.
**2nd row** P1, [K1, P1] to end.
**3rd row** As 2nd row.
**4th row** As 1st row.
These 4 rows form double moss st patt.
Cont in patt until Back measures same as Front to cast off edge, ending with a wrong side row.
**Shape Shoulders**
Cast off 30(31:32) sts at beg of next 2

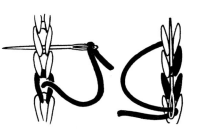

rows. Cast off rem 37(39:43) sts.

## SLEEVES

With 4 mm (No 8/US 5) needles and MC, cast on 47(49:51) sts.
Work 6 cm/2¼ in in double moss st patt as on Back for cuff. Cont in patt, inc one st at each end of 13th row and every foll 4th row until there are 77(81:87) sts, working inc sts into patt.
Cont straight until Sleeve measures 30(33:36)cm 11¾ (13:14¼) in from beg, ending with a wrong side row. Cast off.

## TO MAKE UP

Work Swiss Darning (see diagram) if necessary. Join shoulder seams. Sew on sleeves, placing centre of sleeves to shoulder seams. Join side and sleeve seams, reversing seams on cuffs.

**Swiss Darning.** Bring needle out to front at base of stitch to be covered. Insert needle under the base of stitch above, then back at base. Emerge at base of next stitch to be covered.

### Crochet Edging

With right side facing and crochet hook, join MC yarn to Right Front side seam. Work 1 round of dc (the number of dc should be divisible by 3) along cast on edge of Right Front, along straight front edge, around neck edge and down straight front edge of Left Front, then along cast on edge of Left Front and Back, working 3 dc in every corner, ss in first dc. Fasten off.
**Next round** Join A in same place as ss, *3 ch, 1 dc in first of 3 ch (picot made), miss 2 dc, 1 dc in next dc; rep from * to end. Fasten off. With wrong side of sleeve facing, work crochet edging along lower edge of sleeves. Turn back cuffs. Sew on buttons.

# *Wheatsheaf Sweater*

See Page
29

### MEASUREMENTS

| To fit age | 3–4 | 5–6 | Years |
|---|---|---|---|
| Actual chest measurement | 90 | 94 | **cm** |
| | 35¼ | 37 | **in** |
| Length | 43 | 48 | **cm** |
| | 17 | 19 | **in** |
| Sleeve seam | 26 | 30 | **cm** |
| | 10¼ | 11¾ | **in** |

### MATERIALS

13(14) 50 g balls of Rowan DK Handknit Cotton.
Pair each of 3¼ mm (No 10/US 3) and 4 mm (No 8/US 5) knitting needles.
Cable needle.

### TENSION

20 sts and 28 rows to 10 cm/4 in square over st st on 4 mm (No 8/US 5) needles.

### ABBREVIATIONS

**C4B** = sl next 2 sts onto cable needle and leave at back of work, K2, then K2 from cable needle;
**C4F** = sl next 2 sts onto cable needle and leave at front of work, K2, then K2 from cable needle;
**Cr3L** = sl next 2 sts onto cable needle and leave at front of work, P1, then K2 from cable needle;
**Cr3R** = sl next st onto cable needle and leave at back of work, K2, then P1 from cable needle;
**Cr4L** = sl next 2 sts onto cable needle and leave at front of work, P2, then K2 from cable needle;
**Cr4R** = sl next 2 sts onto cable needle and leave at back of work, K2, then P2 from cable needle;
**MB** = make bobble as follows: [K1, P1, K1, P1, K1, P1, K1] all in next st, pass 2nd, 3rd, 4th, 5th, 6th and 7th sts over first st.
Also see page 5.

### PANEL A – worked over 16 sts.

**1st row** (wrong side) K5, P6, K5.
**2nd row** P5, K2, C4B, P5.
**3rd row** As 1st row.
**4th row** P5, C4B, K2, P5.
**5th to 12th rows** Rep 1st to 4th rows twice.
**13th row** As 1st row.
**14th row** P4, Cr3R, K2, Cr3L, P4.
**15th row** K4, P2, [K1, P2] twice, K4.
**16th row** P3, Cr3R, P1, K2, P1, Cr3L, P3.
**17th row** K3, P2, [K2, P2] twice, K3.
**18th row** P2, Cr3R, P2, K2, P2, Cr3L, P2.
**19th row** K2, P2, [K3, P2] twice, K2.
**20th row** P2, Cr3L, P2, K2, P2, Cr3R, P2.
**21st row** As 17th row.
**22nd row** P3, Cr3L, P1, K2, P1, Cr3R, P3.
**23rd row** As 15th row.
**24th row** P4, Cr3L, K2, Cr3R, P4.
These 24 rows form patt.

### PANEL B – worked over 12 sts.

**1st row** (wrong side) K2, P2, K4, P2, K2.
**2nd row** P2, K2, P4, K2, P2.
**3rd row** As 1st row.
**4th row** P2, Cr4L, Cr4R, P2.
**5th row** K4, P4, K4.
**6th row** P4, Cr4L, P4.
**7th row** K4, P2, K6.
**8th row** P6, Cr3L, P3.
**9th row** K3, P2, K7.
**10th row** P7, Cr3L, P2.

11th row K2, P2, K8.
12th row P3, MB, P4, K2, P2.
13th row As 11th row.
14th row P7, Cr3R, K2.
15th row As 9th row.
16th row P6, Cr3R, P3.
17th row As 7th row.
18th row P4, C4B, P4.
19th row As 5th row.
20th row P2, Cr4R, Cr4L, P2.
21st to 25th rows Work 1st to 5th rows.
26th row P4, Cr4R, P4.
27th row K6, P2, K4.
28th row P3, Cr3R, P6.
29th row K7, P2, K3.
30th row P2, Cr3R, P7.
31st row K8, P2, K2.
32nd row P2, K2, P4, MB, P3.
33rd row As 31st row.
34th row P2, Cr3L, P7.
35th row As 29th row.
36th row P3, Cr3L, P6.
37th row As 27th row.
38th row P4, C4F, P4.
39th row As 5th row.
40th row As 20th row.
These 40 rows form patt.

## BACK
With 3¼ mm (No 10/US 3) needles, cast on 101(107) sts.
1st row (wrong side) K2, [P1 tbl, K2] 6(7) times, * P4, K2, [P1 tbl, K2] 3 times, P4, * K2, [P1 tbl, K2] 7 times, rep from * to *, K2, [P1 tbl, K2] 6(7) times.
2nd row P2, [K1 tbl, P2] 6(7) times, * C4F, P2, [K1 tbl, P2] 3 times, C4B *; P2, [K1 tbl, P2] 7 times, rep from * to *, P2, [K1 tbl, P2] 6(7) times.
3rd row As 1st row.
4th row P2, [K1 tbl, P2] 6(7) times, * K4, P2, [K1 tbl, P2] 3 times, K4 *; P2, [K1 tbl, P2] 7 times, rep from * to *, P2, [K1 tbl, P2] 6(7) times.
These 4 rows form rib patt. Rep them twice more, then work 1st row again.
Inc row [Patt 15(33), m1] 2(1) times, patt 12, [m1, patt 4] 5 times, patt 9, [m1, patt 15(33)] 2(1) times. 110(114) sts.
Change to 4 mm (No 8/US 5) needles.
Work in main patt as follows:
1st row (wrong side) K1, [P1, K1] 2(3) times, work 1st row of Panel A, * P4, work 1st row of Panel B, P4 *; K28, rep from * to *, work 1st row of Panel A, K1, [P1, K1] 2(3) times.
2nd row P1, [K1, P1] 2(3) times, work 2nd row of Panel A, * K4, work 2nd row of Panel B, K4 *; P 28, rep from * to *, work 2nd row of Panel A, P1, [K1, P1] 2(3) times.
3rd row P1, [K1, P1] 2(3) times, work 3rd row of Panel A, * P4, work 3rd row of Panel B, P4 *; K28, rep from * to *, work 3rd row of Panel A, P1, [K1, P1] 2(3) times.
4th row K1, [P1, K1] 2(3) times, work 4th row of Panel A, * C4F, work 4th row of Panel B, C4B *; P28, rep from * to *, work 4th row of Panel A, K1, [P1, K1] 2(3) times.
These 4 rows set position of Panels and form double moss st at sides.
Cont in patt as set until Back measures 43(48) cm/17(19) in from beg, ending with

a wrong side row.
### Shape Shoulders
Cast off 20(21) sts at beg of next 2 rows and 21 sts at beg of foll 2 rows. Leave rem 28(30) sts on a holder.

## FRONT
Work as given for Back until Front measures 36(41) cm/14¼(16¼) in from beg, ending with a wrong side row.
### Shape Neck
Next row Patt 49(50), turn.
Work on this set of sts only. Keeping patt correct, dec one st at neck edge on every row until 41(42) sts rem. Cont straight until Front matches Back to shoulder shaping, ending at side edge.
### Shape Shoulder
Cast off 20(21) sts at beg of next row.
Work 1 row. Cast off rem 21 sts.
With right side facing, slip centre 12(14) sts onto a holder, rejoin yarn to rem sts and patt to end. Complete to match first side.

## SLEEVES
With 3¼ mm (No 10/US 3) needles, cast on 47 sts.
1st row (wrong side) K2, [P1 tbl, K2] 4 times, P4, K2, [P1 tbl, K2] 3 times, P4, K2, [P1 tbl, K2] 4 times.
2nd row P2, [K1 tbl, P2] 4 times, C4F, P2, [K1 tbl, P2] 3 times, C4B, P2, [K1 tbl, P2] 4 times.
3rd row As 1st row.
4th row P2, [K1 tbl, P2] 4 times, K4, P2, [K1 tbl, P2] 3 times, K4, P2, [K1 tbl, P2] 4 times.
These 4 rows form rib patt. Rep them twice more, then work 1st row again.
Inc row Patt 1, m1, [patt 3, m1] 4 times, patt 10, m1, patt 11, [m1, patt 3] 4 times, m1, patt 1. 58 sts.
Change to 4 mm (No 8/US 5) needles.

Work in main patt as follows:
1st row (wrong side) K1, P1, K1, work 1st row of Panel A, P4, work 1st row of Panel B, P4, work 1st row of Panel A, K1, P1, K1.
2nd row P1, K1, P1, work 2nd row of Panel A, K4, work 2nd row of Panel B, K4, work 2nd row of Panel A, P1, K1, P1.
3rd row P1, K1, P1, work 3rd row of Panel A, P4, work 3rd row of Panel B, P4, work 3rd row of Panel A, P1, K1, P1.
4th row K1, P1, K1, work 4th row of Panel A, C4F, work 4th row of Panel B, C4B, work 4th row of Panel A, K1, P1, K1.
These 4 rows set position of Panels and form double moss st at sides.
Cont in patt as set, inc one st at each end of next row and every foll 3rd row until there are 88(92) sts, working inc sts into double moss st.
Cont straight until Sleeve measures 26(30) cm/10¼(11¾) in from beg, ending with a wrong side row. Cast off.

## NECKBAND
Join right shoulder seam.
With 3¼ mm (No 10/US 3) needles and right side facing, pick up and K 21 sts down left front neck, P4(14), [m1, P4] 2(0) times across centre front sts, pick up and K 21 sts up right front neck, [K2(3), m1, K2(3)] 7(5) times across back neck sts. 91 sts.
1st row K1, * P4, K2, [P1 tbl, K2] 3 times; rep from * to end.
2nd row * P2, [K1 tbl, P2] 3 times, K4; rep from * to last st, P1.
3rd row As 1st row.
4th row * P2, [K1 tbl, P2] 3 times, C4F, P2, [K1 tbl, P2] 3 times, C4B; rep from * to last st, P1.
These 4 rows form rib patt. Rep them twice more, then work 1st row again.
Cast off in patt.

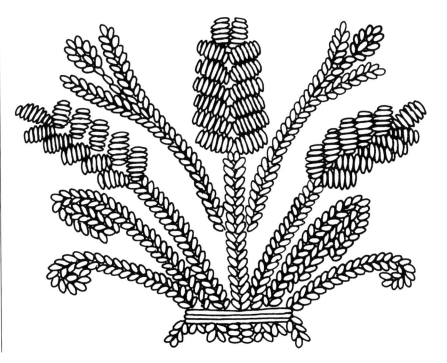

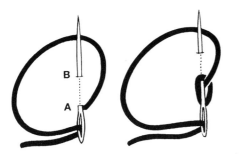

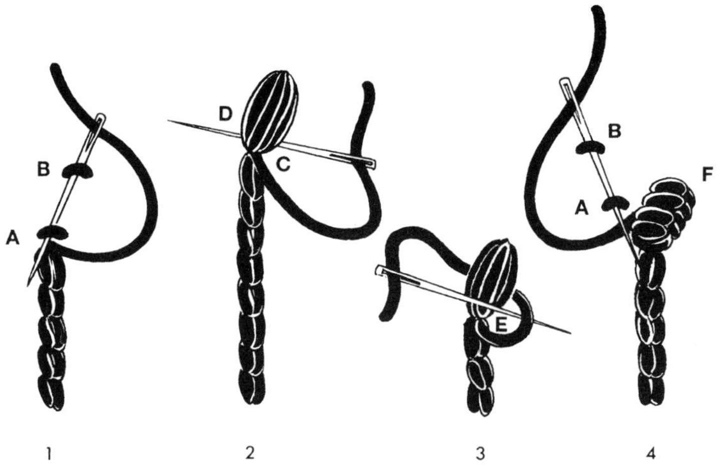

**Chain Stitch.** Bring needle out at A. Insert back at A and emerge at B, looping yarn under the tip of needle. Pull needle through ready for next stitch.

1    2    3    4

## TO MAKE UP
Join left shoulder and neckband seam. Sew on sleeves, placing centre of sleeves to shoulder seams. Join side and sleeve seams. Embroider wheatsheaf as shown on diagram (page 71).
**Wheatsheaf** Work laid threads (diagram 1, above) as follows: bring needle out at

A, * catch loop of knitted st at B, then catch loop of knitted st at A *; rep from * to * 2 or 3 times more.
Couch laid threads (diagram 2 and 3) as follows: * insert needle under laid threads at C and bring out at D, pull through leaving small loop. Insert needle into loop at E and pull up tightly *; rep from * to *

until laid threads are covered, taking care to keep sts close together.
Insert needle at F (diagram 4) and bring needle out at A, laid threads and couch them as before working in reverse direction.

# *Tunic with Pig Motif*

See Page
*31*

### MEASUREMENTS

| To fit age | 2–3 | 3–4 | 4–5 | Years |
|---|---|---|---|---|
| Actual chest measurement | 76 | 82 | 88 | **cm** |
| | 30 | 32¼ | 34¾ | **in** |
| Length | 44 | 47 | 50 | **cm** |
| | 17¼ | 18½ | 19¾ | **in** |
| Sleeve seam | 24 | 27 | 30 | **cm** |
| | 9½ | 10½ | 11¾ | **in** |

### MATERIALS
10(10:11) 50 g balls of Rowan DK Handknit Cotton in Navy (MC).
Small amount of same in each of Pink and Brown.
Pair each of 3¼ mm (No 10/US 3) and 4 mm (No 8/US 5) knitting needles.

### TENSION
20 sts and 28 rows to 10 cm/4 in square over st st on 4 mm (No 8/US 5) needles.

### ABBREVIATIONS
See page 00.

### NOTE
Read Chart from right to left on right side rows and from left to right on wrong side rows. When working motif, use separate lengths of contrast yarn for each coloured area and twist yarns together on wrong side when changing colour to avoid holes.

### POCKET LINING (make one)
With 4 mm (No 8/US 5) needles and MC, cast on 20 sts. Beg with a K row, work 18 rows in st st. Leave these sts on a holder.

### FRONT
Work as given for Back until Front measures 25(27:29) cm/10(10½:11½) in from beg, ending with a P row.
Place motif as follows:
**Next row** K12(16:20)MC, K across 1st row of Chart, K48(50:52)MC.
**Next row** P48(50:52)MC, P across 2nd row of Chart, P12(16:20)MC.
Cont working as set until 14th row of Chart has been worked.
Cont in MC only, work 2 rows.
**Place Pocket**
**Next row** K10(14:18), slip next 20 sts onto a holder, K across sts of pocket lining, K to end.
Cont until Front measures 38(41:44) cm/15(16¼:17½) in from beg, ending with a P row.
**Shape Neck**
**Next row** K32(34:36), turn.

### BACK
With 3¼ mm (No 10/US 3) needles and MC, cast on 70(76:82) sts.
**1st row** (right side) K2(3:2), [P2, K2] to last 0(1:0) st, K0(1:0).
**2nd row** P0(1:0), [P2, K2] to last 2(3:2) sts, P2(3:2).
Rep last 2 rows until work measures 4(4:5) cm/1½ (1½:2) in from beg, ending with a wrong side row.
Change to 4 mm (No 8/US 5) needles.

**Next row** Cast on 3 sts for top of slit, K to end.
**Next row** Cast on 3 sts for top of slit, P to end. 76(82:88) sts.
Cont in st st until work measures 44(47:50) cm/17¼(18½:19¾) in from beg, ending with a P row.
**Shape Shoulders**
Cast off 11(12:13) sts at beg of next 4 rows. Leave rem 32(34:36) sts on a holder.

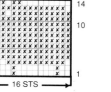

KEY
☐ = Navy
x = Pink
▲ = Brown

Work on this set of sts only. Dec one st at neck edge on every row until 22(24:26) sts rem. Cont straight until Front matches Back to shoulder shaping, ending at side edge.

### Shape Shoulder
Cast off 11(12:13) sts at beg of next row. Work 1 row. Cast off rem 11(12:13) sts. With right side facing, slip centre 12 (14:16) sts onto a holder, rejoin yarn to rem sts and K to end. Complete to match first side.

### SLEEVES
With 3¼ mm (No 10/US 3) needles and MC, cast on 34(38:38) sts. Work 4(5:5) cm/1½ (2:2) in in rib as given for 1st size on Back welt, ending with a 1st row.
**Inc row** Rib 2(3:1), inc in next st, [rib 3(5:4), inc in next st] to last 3(4:1) sts, rib 3(4:1). 42(44:46) sts.
Change to 4 mm (No 8/US 5) needles. Beg with a K row, work in st st, inc one st

at each end of 3rd row and every foll 4th row until there are 66(70:74) sts.
Cont straight for a few rows until Sleeve measures 22(25:28) cm/8¾(9¾:11) in from beg, ending with a P row.
Now work 2 cm/¾ in in rib as given for 1st size on Back welt, ending with a wrong side row. Cast off in rib.

### NECKBAND
Join right shoulder seam.
With 3¼ mm (No 10/US 3) needles, MC and right side facing, pick up and K 21 sts down left front neck, K across centre front sts, pick up and K 21 sts up right front neck, K across back neck sts. 86(90:94) sts. Beg with a 2nd row, work 4 (5:5) cm/1½(2:2) in in rib as given for 1st size on Back welt. Cast off in rib.

### POCKET TOP
With 3¼ mm (No 10/US 3) needles, MC and right side facing, K across sts of

pocket top inc 2 sts evenly across. 22 sts. Beg with a 2nd row, work 5 rows in rib as given for 1st size on Back welt.
Cast off in rib.

### SLIT EDGINGS
With 3¼ mm (No 10/US 3) needles, MC and right side facing, pick up and K 8(8:12) sts from lower edge to cast on sts for top of slit at right side edge of Back. Work 4 rows in P2, K2 rib. Cast off in rib. Work left side of Back to match.
Work Front slit edgings in same way.

### TO MAKE UP
Join left shoulder and neckband seam. Sew on sleeves, placing centre of sleeves to shoulder seams. Join row ends of slit edgings to cast on sts for top of slits. Beginning at top of slits, join side and sleeve seams. Catch down pocket lining and sides of pocket top. Embroider pig's tail in Pink and nostrils in MC.

# Cricket Sweater with Cows

See Page
**31**

| MEASUREMENTS To fit age | 4–6 | Years |
|---|---|---|
| Actual chest measurement | 87 | cm |
|  | 34 | in |
| Length | 49 | cm |
|  | 19¼ | in |
| Sleeve seam | 31 | cm |
|  | 12¼ | in |

### MATERIALS
12 × 50 g balls of Rowan DK Handknit Cotton in Cream (MC).
1 × 50 g ball of same in each of Pale Blue (A), Red (B), Pink (C) and Tan. Small amount of Black for embroidery.
Pair each of 3¼ mm (No 10/US 3) and 4 mm (No 8/US 5) knitting needles.
One 3¼ mm (No 10/US 3) circular needle, 60 cm long.
Cable needle.

### TENSION
28 sts and 30 rows to 10 cm/4 in square over cable pattern on 4 mm (No 8/US 5) needles.

### ABBREVIATIONS
C6F = slip next 3 sts onto cable needle and leave at front of work, K3, then K3 from cable needle.
Also see page 5.

### NOTE
Read Charts from right to left on every round. When working motifs, use separate small balls or lengths of contrast yarns for each coloured area and twist yarns together on wrong side when changing colour to avoid holes.

### BACK
With 3¼ mm (No 10/US 3) needles and MC, cast on 92 sts.
**1st row** (right side) P2, [K2, P1] to end.
**2nd row** [K1, P2] to last 2 sts, K2.
Rep last 2 rows once more. With A, K 1 row, then rep 2nd row.
Cont in MC only, K 1 row. Rib 2 rows.
**Inc row** K1, m1, [P2, m1, K1] to last 4 sts, P2, K2. 122 sts.

Change to 4 mm (No 8/US 5) needles.
Work in cable patt as follows:
**1st row** (right side) P2, [K6, P2] to end.
**2nd row** K2, [P6, K2] to end.
**3rd and 4th rows** As 1st and 2nd rows.
**5th row** P2, [C6F, P2] to end.
**6th row** As 2nd row.
**7th to 10th rows** Rep 1st and 2nd rows twice.
These 10 rows form patt. Cont in patt until

Back measures 40 cm/15¾ in from beg, ending with a wrong side row.
### Shape Neck
**Next row** Patt 48, turn.
Work on this set of sts only. Keeping patt correct, dec one st at neck edge until 22 sts rem. Patt 1 row. Cast off.
With right side facing, slip centre 26 sts onto a holder, rejoin yarn to rem sts and patt to end. Complete to match first side.

### FRONT
Work as given for Back until Front measures 22 cm/8½ in from beg, ending with a wrong side row.
### Shape Neck
**Next row** Patt 59, work 2 tog, turn.
Work on this set of sts only. Dec one st at neck edge on every foll alt row until 22 sts rem. Cont straight until Front measures same as Back to cast off edge, ending with a wrong side row. Cast off.
With right side facing, rejoin yarn to rem sts, work 2 tog, patt to end. Complete to match first side.

### SLEEVES
With 3¼ mm (No 10/US 3) needles and MC, cast on 38 sts.
**1st row** (right side) P2, [K2, P1] to end.
**2nd row** [K1, P2] to last 2 sts, K2.
Rep last 2 rows once more. With B, K 1 row, then rep 2nd row.
Cont in MC only, K 1 row. Rib 4 rows.
**Inc row** K1, m1, [P2, m1, K1] to last 4 sts, P2, K2. 50 sts.
Change to 4 mm (No 8/US 5) needles. Work in cable patt as given for Back, **at the same time**, inc one st at each end of 9 foll 3rd rows, then on every foll 4th row until there are 88 sts, working inc sts into patt. Cont straight until Sleeve measures

31 cm/12¼ in from beg, ending with a wrong side row. Cast off.

## NECKBAND
Join shoulder seams.
With 3¼ mm (No 10/US 3) circular needle, MC and right side facing, pick up and K 80 sts up right front neck, 26 sts down right back neck, K2 tog, [K6, K2 tog] 3 times across centre back sts, pick up and K 26 sts up left back neck and 80 sts down left front neck. 234 sts.
**Next round** Sl 1, K1, psso, P2, [K2, P2] to last 2 sts, K2 tog.
**Next round** Sl 1, K1, psso, P1, [K2, P2] to last 5 sts, K2, P1, K2 tog.
**Next 3 rounds** With A, sl 1, K1, psso, K to last 2 sts, K2 tog. 224 sts.
Work motifs as follows:
**Next round** With A, sl 1, K1, psso, K15, * K across 1st row of Chart 1, K3A, K across 1st row of Chart 1 *; K1A, K across 1st row of Chart 2, K7A, [K across 1st row of Chart 2, K4A] 4 times, K3A, K across 1st row of Chart 2, K1A, rep from * to *, with A, K15, K2 tog.
**Next round** With A, sl 1, K1, psso, patt 71, [with A, K2 tog, sl 1, K1, psso, patt 14] 5 times, patt 57, with A, K2 tog.
Work 3 rounds, dec 2 sts at centre front only on every round.
**Next round** With A, sl 1, K1, psso, patt 66, [with A, K2 tog, sl 1, K1, psso, patt 12] 5 times, patt 54, with A, K2 tog.
Work 3 rounds, dec 2 sts at centre front only on every round.

**Next round** With A, sl 1, K1, psso, patt 61, [with A, K2 tog, sl 1, K1, psso, patt 10] 5 times, patt 51, with A, K2 tog.
**Next round** With A, sl 1, K1, psso, patt 44, with A, K to last 46 sts, patt 43, with A, K2 tog.
Work 2 rounds, dec 2 sts at centre front only on every round.
**Next round** With A, sl 1, K1, psso, patt 41, with A, K15, [K2 tog, sl 1, K1, psso, K8A] 5 times, K7A, patt 41, with A, K2 tog.
Work 2 rounds in A, dec 2 sts at centre front only on every round.
**Next round** With A, [sl 1, K1, psso, K7] 6 times, [K2 tog, sl 1, K1, psso, K6] 4 times, K2 tog, sl 1, K1, psso, [K7, K2 tog] 6 times. 130 sts.
**Next round** With MC, sl 1, K1, psso, K to last 2 sts, K2 tog.

**Next round** With MC, sl 1, K1, psso, K1, [P2, K2] to last 5 sts, P2, K1, K2 tog.
**Next round** With MC, sl 1, K1, psso, [P2, K2] to last 4 sts, P2, K2 tog.
**Next round** With C, sl 1, K1, psso, K to last 2 sts, K2 tog.
**Next round** With C, sl 1, K1, psso, [K2, P2] to last 4 sts, K2, K2 tog.
**Next round** With MC, sl 1, K1, psso, K to last 2 sts, K2 tog.
**Next round** With MC, sl 1, K1, psso, [P2, K2] to last 4 sts, P2, K2 tog.
With MC, cast off in rib, dec as before.

## TO MAKE UP
Sew on sleeves, placing centre of sleeves to shoulder seams. Join side and sleeve seams. With Black, embroider eyes on cow motifs.

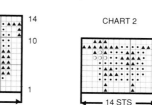

CHART 1
CHART 2

KEY
□ = Pale Blue
▲ = Tan
• = Cream
○ = Pink

# *Hearts and Hens Sweater*

See Page
*32*

| MEASUREMENTS To fit age | 18–24 | 24–36 | Months |
|---|---|---|---|
| Actual chest measurement | 75 | 81 | cm |
| | 29½ | 32 | in |
| Length | 38 | 41 | cm |
| | 15 | 16 | in |
| Sleeve seam | 22 | 24 | cm |
| | 8½ | 9½ | in |

## MATERIALS
5(6) 50 g balls of Rowan DK Handknit Cotton in Light Blue (MC).
1(1) 50 g ball of same in each of Pink, Red, Cream, Dark Blue and Brown.
Pair each of 3¼ mm (No 10/US 3) and 4 mm (No 8/US 5) knitting needles.

## TENSION
20 sts and 28 rows to 10 cm/4 in square over st st on 4 mm (No 8/US 5) needles.

## ABBREVIATIONS
See page 5.

## NOTE
Read Chart from right to left on right side rows and from left to right on wrong side rows. Use separate lengths or small balls of yarn for each coloured area and twist yarns together on wrong side when changing colour to avoid holes.

## BACK
With 3¼ mm (No 10/US 3) needles and MC, cast on 74(78) sts.
**1st row** (right side) K2, [P2, K2] to end.
**2nd row** P2, [K2, P2] to end.
Rep last 2 rows until work measures 3(4) cm/1¼(1½) in from beg, ending with a 2nd row and inc 1(3) sts evenly across last row. 75(81) sts.
Change to 4 mm (No 8/US 5) needles.
Beg with a K row, work in st st and patt from Chart until 100th(104th) row of Chart has been worked.
Cont in MC only.
### Shape Shoulders
Cast off 12(13) sts at beg of next 4 rows. Leave rem 27(29) sts on a holder.

## FRONT
Work as given for Back until 84th row of Chart has been worked.
### Shape Neck
**Next row** Patt 30(32), turn.
Work on this set of sts only. Keeping patt correct, dec one st at neck edge on every row until 24(26) sts rem. Cont straight until 100th(104th) row of Chart has been worked.
Cont in MC only.

## Shape Shoulder

Cast off 12(13) sts at beg of next row.
Work 1 row. Cast off rem 12(13) sts.
With right side facing, slip centre 15(17)
sts onto a holder, rejoin yarn to rem sts
and patt to end. Complete to match first
side, reversing shoulder shaping.

## SLEEVES

With 3¼ mm (No 10/US 3) needles and
MC, cast on 34(38) sts.
Work 4(5) cm/1½(2) in in rib as given for
Back welt, ending with a 1st row.
Inc row Rib 2(3), inc in next st, [rib 4, inc
in next st] 6 times, rib 1(4). 41(45) sts.
Change to 4 mm (No 8/US 5) needles.

Beg with a K row, work in st st and patt
from Chart, inc one st at each end of
every 3rd row until there are 71(75) sts,
omitting pig and cow motifs. Patt 5(9)
rows straight. Cast off.

## NECKBAND

Join right shoulder seam.
With 3¼ mm (No 10/US 3) needles, MC
and right side facing, pick up and K 19
(21) sts down left front neck, K across
centre front sts dec one st, pick up and K
19(21) sts up right front neck, K across
back neck sts dec one st. 78(86) sts. Beg
with a 2nd row, work 9 rows in rib as
given for Back welt. Beg with a K row,

work 4 rows in st st. Cast off.

## TO MAKE UP

Join left shoulder and neckband seam,
reversing seam on last 4 rows of
neckband. Allow the top of neckband to
roll back. Sew on sleeves, placing centre
of sleeves to shoulder seams. Join side
and sleeve seams. Embroider pigs' tails
with Pink and nostrils with Dark Blue. With
Red, work 2 lazy daisy stitches (see
diagram page 54) on hens heads for
comb. Embroider beak, legs and feet on
each hen with Red and straight stitch (see
diagram page 56).

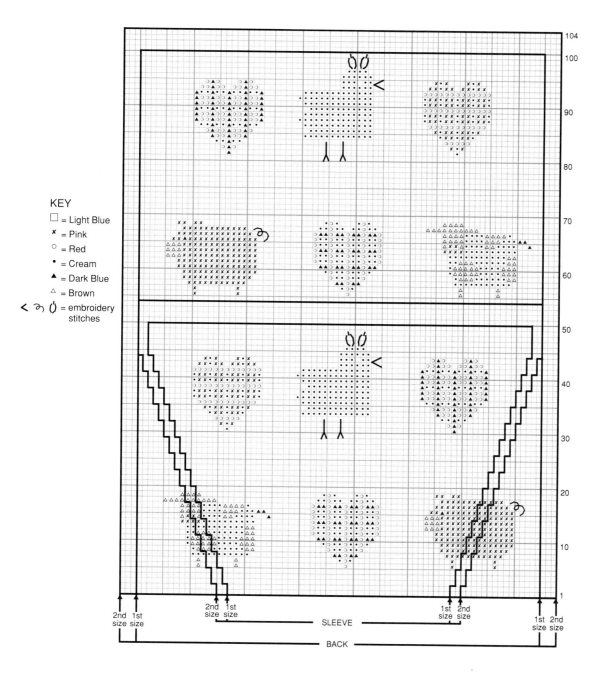

KEY
□ = Light Blue
x = Pink
○ = Red
• = Cream
▲ = Dark Blue
△ = Brown
< ⁊ ◊ = embroidery stitches

SLEEVE

BACK

# Sampler Sweater

See Page
*33*

**MEASUREMENTS**

| To fit age | 3–4 | 5–6 | Years |
|---|---|---|---|
| Actual chest measurement | 84 | 89 | **cm** |
| | 33 | 35 | **in** |
| Length to shoulder | 45 | 49 | **cm** |
| | 17¾ | 19¼ | **in** |
| Sleeve seam | 26 | 29 | **cm** |
| | 10¼ | 11½ | **in** |

## MATERIALS
8(9) 50 g balls of Rowan Designer DK Wool in Steel (MC).
1(1) 50 g ball of same in each of Cream (A) and Red (B).
Pair each of 3¼ mm (No 10/US 3) and 4 mm (No 8/US 5) knitting needles.

## TENSION
23 sts and 33 rows to 10 cm/4 in square over patt on 4 mm (No 8/US 5) needles.

## ABBREVIATIONS
**MB** = make bobble, K into front, back, front and back of next st, turn, P4, turn, K4, turn, [K2 tog] twice, turn, K2 tog.
Also see page 5.

## NOTE
Read Charts from right to left on right side rows and from left to right on wrong side rows. Use separate lengths of A and B yarn for each motif and twist yarns together on wrong side when changing colour to avoid holes. If preferred the motifs may be Swiss Darned when knitting is complete.

## BOBBLE PATTERN – worked over 17 sts.
**1st row** (right side) K17.
**2nd row and every alt row** P17.
**3rd row** K8, MB, K8.
**5th row** K17.
**7th row** K5, MB, K5, MB, K5.
**9th row** K17.
**11th row** K2, [MB, K5] twice, MB, K2.
**13th row** K17.
**15th row** As 7th row.
**17th row** K17.
**19th row** As 3rd row.
**20th row** P17.
These 20 rows form Bobble patt.

## BACK
With 3¼ mm (No 10/US 3) needles and MC, cast on 97(103) sts. K 13(15) rows. Change to 4 mm (No 8/US 5) needles. Work in patt as follows:
**1st row** (right side) K2(3)MC, K across 1st row of Chart 1, * with MC, K2(3), work 1st row of Bobble patt, K2(3)*; K across 1st row of Chart 2, rep from * to *, K across 1st row of Chart 3, K2(3)MC.
**2nd row** K2(3)MC, P across 2nd row of Chart 3, * with MC, K2(3), work 2nd row of Bobble patt, K2(3)*; P across 2nd row of Chart 2, rep from * to *, P across 2nd row of Chart 1, K2(3)MC.
**3rd to 20th rows** Rep last 2 rows 9 times but working 3rd to 20th rows of Bobble patt and Charts.
**21st to 24th(26th) rows** With MC, K.
**25th(27th) row** * With MC, K2(3), work 1st row of Bobble patt, k2(3)*; K across 1st row of Chart 4, rep from * to *, K across 1st row of Chart 5, rep from * to *.

**26th(28th) row** * With MC, K2(3), work 2nd row of Bobble patt, K2(3)*; P across 2nd row of Chart 5, rep from * to *, P across 2nd row of Chart 4, rep from * to *.
**27th(29th) to 44th(46th) rows** Work as 3rd to 20th rows.
**45th(47th) to 48th(52nd) rows** With MC, K.
**49th(53rd) to 72nd(78th) rows** Work as 1st to 24th(26th) rows but working from Chart 6 instead of Chart 1, Chart 7 instead of Chart 2 and Chart 1 instead of Chart 3.
**73rd(79th) to 96th(104th) rows** Work as 25th(27th) to 48th(52nd) rows but working from Chart 3 instead of Chart 4 and Chart 4 instead of Chart 5.

**97th(105th) to 120th(130th) rows** Work as 1st to 24th(26th) rows but working from Chart 2 instead of Chart 1, Chart 5 instead of Chart 2 and Chart 6 instead of Chart 3.
**121st(131st) to 140th(150th) rows** Work as 25th(27th) to 44th(46th) rows but working from Chart 7 instead of Chart 4 and Chart 1 instead of Chart 5.
With MC, K 2(4) rows. Cast off.

## FRONT
Work as Back until Front measures 16(18) rows less than Back to cast off edge, ending with a wrong side row.
**Shape Neck**
**Next row** Patt 43(45) sts and turn.
Work on this set of sts only. Keeping patt correct, dec one st at neck edge on next 11 rows. Patt 4(6) rows straight. Cast off rem 32(34) sts.
With right side facing, rejoin yarn to rem sts, cast off centre 11(13) sts, patt to end.
Complete to match first side.

## SLEEVES
With 3¼ mm (No 10/US 3) needles and MC, cast on 43(45) sts.
**1st row** (right side) K1, [P1, K1] to end.
**2nd row** P1, [K1, P1] to end.
Rep last 2 rows until work measures 4(5) cm/1½ (2) in from beg, ending with a right side row.
**Inc row** Rib 1(3), [inc in next st, rib 3, inc in next st, rib 2] to end. 55(57) sts.
Change to 4 mm (No 8/US 5) needles. Work in patt as follows:
**1st row** K across 1st row of Chart 1, with MC, K2(3), work 1st row of Bobble patt, K2(3), K across 1st row of Chart 2.
**2nd row** P across 2nd row of Chart 2, with MC, K2(3), work 2nd row of Bobble patt, K2(3), P across 2nd row of Chart 1.
These 2 rows set position of patt. Cont in patt as set, **at the same time**, inc one st at each end of 3rd row and every foll 4th row until there are 85(89) sts, working inc sts

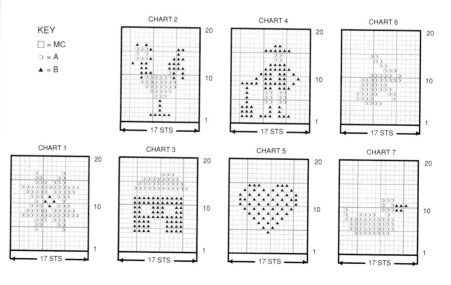

into patt to match Back. Patt 11(13) rows straight. Cast off.

## COLLAR
With 3¼ mm (No 10/US 3) needles and MC, cast on 86(90) sts.

Work 8(9) cm/3(3½) in in garter st (every row K). Cast off loosely.

## TO MAKE UP
Work Swiss Darning (see diagram page 70) if necessary. With B, embroider each

cockerel's beak. Join shoulder seams. Sew on sleeves, placing centre of sleeves to shoulder seams. Beginning at top of welt, join side and sleeve seams. Sew cast on edge of collar to neck edge, beginning and ending at centre front.

# Milk-Maid Sweater

See Page 34

| MEASUREMENTS To fit age | 3–4 | Years |
|---|---|---|
| Actual chest measurement | 92 | cm |
|  | 36¼ | in |
| Length | 42 | cm |
|  | 16½ | in |
| Sleeve seam | 33 | cm |
|  | 13 | in |

## MATERIALS
9 × 50 g balls of Rowan DK Handknit Cotton in Cream (MC).
1 × 50 g ball of same in each of Brown, Pink, Green, Yellow, Light Blue and Dark Blue.
Pair each of 3¼ mm (No 10/US 3) and 4 mm (No 8/US 5) knitting needles.
Set of four 3¼ mm (No 10/US 3) double pointed knitting needles.

## TENSION
20 sts and 28 rows to 10 cm/4 in square over st st on 4 mm (No 8/US 5) needles.

## ABBREVIATIONS
See page 5.

## NOTE
Read Charts from right to left on right side rows and from left to right on wrong side rows. When working motifs, use separate lengths of contrast yarns for each coloured area and twist yarns together on wrong side when changing colour to avoid holes.

K1MC.
**31st to 56th rows** Work 3rd to 28th rows.
**57th row** K1MC, K across 1st row of Chart 3, K2MC, K across 1st row of Chart 4, K2MC, K across 1st row of Chart 5, K2MC, K across 1st row of Chart 6, K1MC.
**58th row** K1MC, P across 2nd row of Chart 6, K2MC, P across 2nd row of Chart 5, K2MC, P across 2nd row of Chart 4, K2MC, P across 2nd row of Chart 3, K1MC.
**59th to 84th rows** Work 3rd to 28th rows.
**85th to 112th rows** Work 1st to 28th rows.
**Shape Shoulders**
**Next row** With MC, cast off 29 sts, K to last 29 sts, cast off last 29 sts.
Leave rem 34 sts on a holder.

## FRONT
Work as given for Back until Front measures 20 rows less than Back to shoulder shaping, ending with a wrong side row.
**Shape Neck**
**Next row** Patt 38, turn.
Work on this set of sts only. Keeping patt correct, cast off 3 sts at beg of next row.

## BACK
With 3¼ mm (No 10/US 3) needles and MC, cast on 86 sts.
Work 5 cm /2 in in K1, P1 rib.
**Inc row** Rib 10, inc in next st, [rib 12, inc in next st] to last 10 sts, rib 10. 92 sts.
Change to 4 mm (No 8/US 5) needles.
Work in patt as follows:
**1st row** (right side) K1MC, K across 1st row of Chart 1, K2MC, K across 1st row of Chart 2, K2MC, K across 1st row of Chart 3, K2MC, K across 1st row of Chart 4, K1MC.
**2nd row** K1MC, P across 2nd row of Chart 4, K2MC, P across 2nd row of Chart 3, K2MC, P across 2nd row of Chart 2, K2MC, P across 2nd row of Chart 1, K1MC.
**3rd to 24th rows** Rep last 2 rows 11 times more but working 3rd to 24th rows of Charts.
**25th to 28th rows** With MC, K.
**29th row** K1MC, K across 1st row of Chart 5, K2MC, K across 1st row of Chart 6, K2MC, K across 1st row of Chart 1, K2MC, K across 1st row of Chart 2, K1MC.
**30th row** K1MC, P across 2nd row of Chart 2, K2MC, P across 2nd row of Chart 1, K2MC, P across 2nd row of Chart 6, K2MC, P across 2nd row of Chart 5,

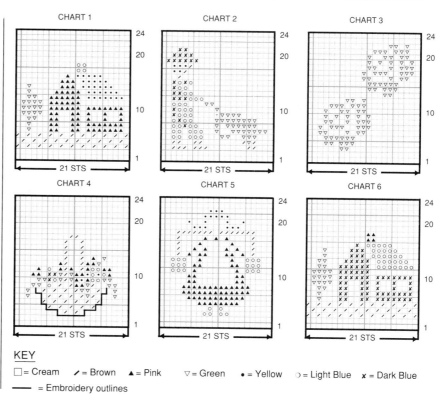

KEY

□ = Cream    ✎ = Brown    ▲ = Pink    ▽ = Green    • = Yellow    ◡ = Light Blue    x = Dark Blue

___ = Embroidery outlines

Dec one st at neck edge on every row until 29 sts rem.
Cont straight until Front matches Back to shoulder shaping, ending with a wrong side row. Cast off.
With right side facing, slip centre 16 sts onto a holder, rejoin yarn to rem sts and patt to end. Patt 1 row. Complete to match first side.

### SLEEVES
With 3¼ mm (No 10/US 3) needles and MC, cast on 46 sts.
Work 5 cm/2 in in K1, P1 rib.
Inc row Rib 1, [inc in next st, rib 4] to end. 55 sts.
Change to 4 mm (No 8/US 5) needles. Work in patt as follows:
1st row (right side) K17MC, K across 1st row of Chart 1, K17MC.
2nd row P15MC, K2MC, P across 2nd row of Chart 1, K2MC, P15MC.
Work a further 22 rows as set, inc one st at each end of 2nd row and 4 foll 5th rows, working inc sts in MC. With MC, K 4

rows, inc one st at each end of last row. 67 sts.
29th row K across 1st row of Chart 2, K2MC, K across 1st row of Chart 3, K2MC, K across 1st row of Chart 4.
30th row P across 2nd row of Chart 4, K2MC, P across 2nd row of Chart 3, K2MC, P across 2nd row of Chart 2.
Work a further 22 rows as set, inc one st at each end of 2nd row and 4 foll 5th rows, working first 2 inc sts into MC and garter st (every row K) and last 3 inc sts in MC and st st. With MC, K 4 rows, inc one st at each end of last row. 79 sts.
57th row K6MC, K across 1st row of Chart 5, K2MC, K across 1st row of Chart 6, K2MC, K across 1st row of Chart 1, K6MC.
58th row P4MC, K2MC, P across 2nd row of Chart 1, K2MC, P across 2nd row of Chart 6, K2MC, P across 2nd row of Chart 5, K2MC, P4MC.
Work a further 22 rows as set. With MC, K 4 rows. Cast off.

### COLLAR
Join shoulder seams.
With right side facing, slip first 8 sts from centre front holder onto a safety pin, join MC yarn and using set of four 3¼ mm (No 10/US 3) double pointed needles, K rem 8 sts, pick up and K 16 sts up right front neck, K back neck sts, pick up and K 16 sts down left front neck, then K8 from safety pin. 82 sts. Work 5 rounds in K1, P1 rib. Turn and work backwards and forwards as follows:
Next row K2, rib to last 2 sts, K2.
Next row K2, m1, rib to last 2 sts, m1, K2.
Rep last 2 rows 8 times more, then work first of the 2 rows again.
Cast off loosely in rib.

### TO MAKE UP
Sew on sleeves, placing centre of sleeves to shoulder seams. Join side and sleeve seams. With Brown, outline base of each basket and embroider face features on each girl.

# *Alphabet Sweater*

See Page
35

| MEASUREMENTS | | |
| --- | --- | --- |
| **To fit age** | **4–6** | **Years** |
| Actual chest measurement | 83 | cm |
| | 32½ | in |
| Length | 48 | cm |
| | 19 | in |
| Sleeve seam | 28 | cm |
| | 11 | in |

### MATERIALS
7 × 50 g balls of Rowan Designer DK Wool in Cream (MC).
1 × 50 g ball of same in each of Rust, Dark Blue, Green, Brown, Grey, Navy, Red, Light Blue and Beige.
Pair each of 3¼ mm (No 10/US 3) and 4 mm (No 8/US 5) knitting needles.

### TENSION
24 sts and 32 rows to 10 cm/4 in square over st st on 4 mm (No 8/US 5) needles.

### ABBREVIATIONS
See page 5.

### NOTE
Read Charts from right to left on right side rows and from left to right on wrong side rows. When working in pattern from Chart 1, strand yarn not in use loosely across wrong side to keep fabric elastic. When working in pattern from Chart 2, use separate small balls or lengths of contrast yarn for each coloured area and twist yarns together on wrong side when changing colour to avoid holes.

### BACK
With 3¼ mm (No 10/US 3) needles and MC, cast on 100 sts. K 13 rows.
Change to 4 mm (No 8/US 5) needles. Beg with a K row, work in st st and patt from Chart 1 until 25th row of Chart 1 has been worked. Cont in st st and patt from Chart 2 until 97th row of Chart 2 has been worked.
Cont in st st and MC only until work

measures 48 cm/19 in from beg, ending with a P row.
Shape Shoulders
Cast off 34 sts at beg of next 2 rows. Cast off rem 32 sts.

### FRONT
Work as given for Back until 85th row of Chart 2 has been worked.

Shape Neck
Next row Patt 44, turn.
Work on this set of sts only. Cont working in patt from Chart 2, dec one st at neck edge on every row until 34 sts rem. Patt 1 row. Cont in st st and MC only until Front matches Back to shoulder shaping, ending at side edge. Cast off.
With right side facing, rejoin yarn to rem sts, cast off centre 12 sts, patt to end. Complete to match first side.

### SLEEVES
With 3¼ mm (No 10/US 3) needles and MC, cast on 44 sts. Work 4 cm/1¼ in in K1, P1 rib.
Inc row Rib 5, [inc in next st, rib 2] to last 3 sts, rib 3. 56 sts.
Change to 4 mm (No 8/US 5) needles. Beg with a K row, work in st st and patt from Chart 2 until 72nd row of Chart 2 has been worked, **at the same time**, inc one st at each end of 3rd row and every foll 4th row until there are 86 sts, working inc sts into patt. Cast off.

### COLLAR
With 3¼ mm (No 10/US 3) needles and MC, cast on 86 sts. Work 8 cm/3 in in garter st (every row K). Cast off loosely.

### TO MAKE UP
Join shoulder seams. Sew on sleeves, placing centre of sleeves to shoulder seams. Beg at top of welt, join side seams then sleeve seams. Sew cast on edge of collar to neck edge, beginning and ending at centre front, then join collar together for first 2 cm/¾ in. With Navy, embroider cockerels' beaks.

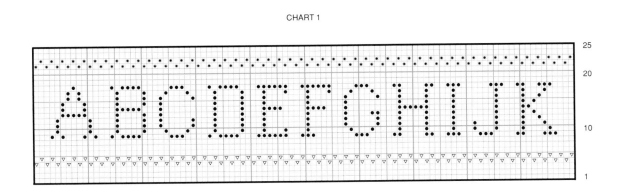

CHART 1

CHART 2

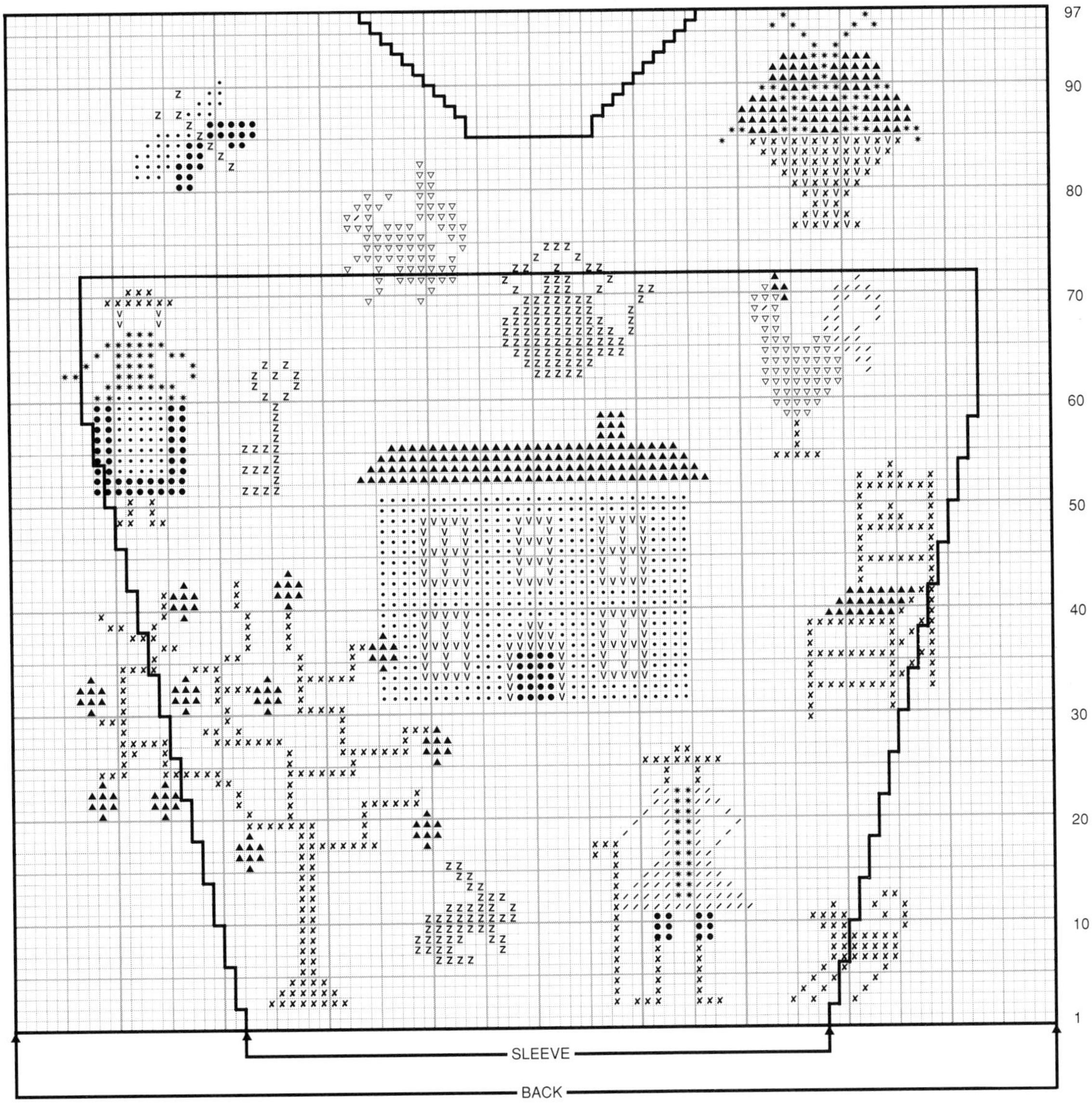

SLEEVE

BACK

KEY

| | | | |
|---|---|---|---|
| □ = Cream | ● = Dark Blue | x = Brown | ╱ = Navy | • = Light blue |
| ▽ = Rust | ∗ = Green | z = Grey | ▲ = Red | v = Beige |

# Source Guide

**Rowan Yarn Addresses**
Rowan yarns are widely available in yarn shops. For details of stockists and mail order sources of Rowan yarns, please write or contact the distributors listed below.
For advice on how to use a substitute yarn, see page 5.

**UNITED KINGDOM**
**Rowan Yarns**, Green Lane Mill, Holmfirth, West Yorkshire, England HD7 1RE.
Tel: (0484) 681881

**USA**
**Westminster Trading Corporation**, 5 Northern Boulevard, Amherst, NH 03031.
Tel: (603) 886 5041/5043

**AUSTRALIA**
**Rowan (Australia)**, 191 Canterbury Road, Canterbury, Victoria 3126.
Tel: (03) 830 1609

**BELGIUM**
**Hedera**, Pleinstraat 68, 3001 Leuven.
Tel: (016) 23 21 89

**CANADA**
**Estelle Designs & Sales Ltd**
Unit 65 & 67, 2220 Midland Avenue, Scarborough, Ontario, M1P 3E6.
Tel: (416) 298 9922

**DENMARK**
**Designer Garn** Vesterbro 33 A, DK-9000 Aalborg.
Tel: (8) 98 13 48 24

**FRANCE**
**Sidel,** Ch Depart, 14C 13840 Rognes.
Tel: (33) 42 50 15 06

**GERMANY**
**Christoph Fritzsch GmbH,**
Gewerbepark Dogelmuhle, D-6367 Karben 1.
Tel: 06039 2071

**HOLLAND**
**Henk & Henrietta Beukers,** Dorpsstraat 9, NL-5327 AR, Hurwenen.
Tel: 04182 1764

**ICELAND**
**Stockurinn,** Kjorgardi, Laugavegi 59, ICE-101 Reykjavik.
Tel: (01) 18258

**ITALY**
**La Compagnia del Cotone,** Via Mazzini 44, 1-10123 Torino.
Tel: (011) 87 83 81

**JAPAN**
**Diakeito Co Ltd,** 2-3-11 Senba-Higashi, Minoh City, Osaka 562.
Tel: 0727 27 6604

**MEXICO**
**Rebecca Pick Estambresy Tejidos Finos S.A. de C.V.,** A.V. Michoacan 30-A, Local 3 Esq Av Mexico, Col Hipodromo Condesa 06170, Mexico 11.
Tel: (05) 2 64 84 74

**NEW ZEALAND**
**John Q Goldingham Ltd,** PO Box 45083, Epuni Railway, Lower Hutt, Wellington,North Island.
Tel: (04) 5674 085

**NORWAY**
**Eureka,** PO Box 357, N-1401 Ski.
Tel: (64) 86 55 70

**SWEDEN**
**Wincent,** Sveavagen 94, 113 58 Stockholm.
Tel: (08) 673 70 60